R E V E L A T I O N

REVELATION

St. John the Divine's Prophecies for the Apocalypse and Beyond

Peter Lorie

*"Life lies
always at some
frontier, making sorties
into the unknown; its path
leads always further into truth.
We cannot call it trackless waste,
because as the path appears it seems
to have lain there awaiting the
steps... thus the surprises,
thus the continuity."*

M.C. Richards

SIMON & SCHUSTER

New York London Toronto Sydney Tokyo Singapore

SIMON & SCHUSTER
Simon & Schuster Building
Rockerfeller Center
1230 Avenue of the Americas
New York, NY 10020

A LABYRINTH BOOK
Copyright © 1994 Labyrinth Publishing (UK) Ltd
Text copyright © 1994 Peter Lorie
Original Illustrations copyright © 1994 Labyrinth Publishing (UK) Ltd

REVELATION was produced by Labyrinth Publishing (UK) Ltd
Design by DW Design
Typesetting by DW Design in London, England

Printed in Singapore by Singapore National Printers
10 9 8 7 6 5 4 3 2 1

Lorie, Peter
      Revelation : the prophecies, the apocalyse, and beyond / Peter Lorie
          p. cm.
      Includes bibliographical references and index.
      ISBN 0-671-88872-2
      1. Bible. N.T. Revelation--Criticism, interpretation, etc.
  I. Title.
  BS2825.2.L87 1994
  228'.06--dc20   93-49383
                                       CIP

Contents

INTRODUCTION

"Write the things which thou hast seen,
and the things which are,
and the things which shall be hereafter…"

Revelation Ch. 1 : 1

THERE ARE MANY WHO BELIEVE THAT THE END OF THE MILLENNIUM WILL bring the Apocalypse predicted in the Book of Revelation – a negative and unhappy apocalypse. It will occur, they believe, as the result of a massive "War to end all Wars," after which a few chosen individuals will meet the "Second Coming" of the Messiah on earth. And this will be the Last Judgment before heaven and hell.

Much of this anticipation has been created over the centuries by the very belief systems that engendered the pessimism in the first place. A great many people on earth are very saddened indeed by what they see around them, what they learn to expect, what they come to believe in, or rather fail to believe in. We, in the West, feel that we have fallen from Grace, and that the salvation offered by organized religion lies in forces outside our control – a form of spiritual disenfranchisement.

The daily demands of a stressful society perhaps also encourages a negative outlook, out of which arises a tendency towards a roundelay of spiraling "dis-affection."

So, when we read the prophetic vision of the Book of Revelation we see largely only the words that support this disillusion – doom and disaster, despondency, and culmination in a judgment of the end of everything, especially us! But actually, this may not have been the original intention. When Jesus and others like him – Buddha, Mahavira, Lao Tzu – spoke about apocalypse or enlightenment, they spoke positively and with joy. They spoke with "affection" – the affection described by the Eastern master U.G. Krishnamurti when he literally felt the pain suffered by a small boy whom he watched being thrashed by his mother – for this affection is truly all you need: the ability to affect and be affected by your world.

Frontispiece: St. John on Patmos experiencing the vision of the apocalypse. Detail from an altarpiece by Hans Memling in St. John's Hospital in Bruges, Belgium.

Below: **The Great Day of His Wrath**, a late Victorian view, by C. Mottram. God's power has long been seen as destructive, giving artists ample opportunity to express their own expectations of the end of the world.

Opposite: Desert road, Monument Valley, Utah.

This dramatic millennial scenario has been awaited for many centuries by many different sects and creeds, and in fact they may all be right. The "end of the world" that was predicted by our Christian fathers will inevitably occur, though not in the form that is commonly expected.

It is the purpose then of this book to show, in its fresh interpretation of St. John's Revelation, that the apocalypse is a revelation of truth that leads to joy, and that the end of the world as we know it is occurring within each individual right now, as a war to end all wars. And the outside world will be the manifestation of that apocalypse. For the word "apocalypse" does not mean disaster or "end of the world," but is the Greek for "revelation," and the revelation of truth is only frightening when we don't know what it is.

There is no doubt that through this revealing of the truth, the world will change dramatically, and St. John's Apocalypse is an extraordinary and clear prophecy of that truth, and of the process by which we reach it. Its brush strokes are both broad and sweeping, with grand, often highly evolved, spiritual notions, and at the same time frequently detailed and down-to-earth, with predictions related to economic changes, political transformation and human psychological awareness. In the following pages we will find much of both.

But the world is probably not going to end in the manner that so many of us fear, for human existence continues on its own behalf because the joint energies of humanity, the group consciousness of us all, is still single-minded enough to wish it to be so, and it is the "single mind" that keeps the dream alive. Whether we believe in an external God or have learned to appreciate that within each of us is our own god, the result is the same. Human life has only just begun, and, according to this interpretation of the apostle John, son of Zebedee, there is far to go yet before we die.

The Book

T HE REVELATION OF ST. JOHN THE DIVINE HAS BEEN AN ENIGMA TO mankind since the Bible first appeared. The last book in the New Testament, it is believed by many Christians to be a message from God containing letters and a series of prophecies which relate to a time in the future – to the "end of the world" as we have known it. Many have interpreted its forecasts to be relevant to the last years of this millennium, when, it is believed, we will all face the final apocalypse. As the early twentieth-century philosopher and teacher Rudolf Steiner discussed in his lectures on The Book of Revelation, the word "revelation" in the context of the Bible is intended to mean "the uncovering of that which has hitherto been hidden," and if we look a little more closely at the contents of Revelation, we find that there is much beneath the surface which indicates such an apocalyptic transformation. In fact, there have been numerous interpretations dating the apocalypse to all sorts of different times in our past, none of which have been fulfilled.

This illustrated interpretation of the text taken from the King James version of the Bible creates a series of pictures of the overall scenario that John's supposed vision implies. Using contemporary photographs and illustrations, this book is designed to help us visualize a picture of the future which builds upon the predictions and provides a developing pattern of how the world could look as the so-called apocalypse transforms us.

The author and philosopher F. Aster Barnwell in his book Meditations on the Apocalypse, has illustrated convincingly that part of the text of the biblical Revelation contains astrological symbolism, so the interpretations in this book will use astrological interpretations and symbols giving, where possible, an indication of the character of the changes and events prophesied by the story written down by John, and perhaps by others who worked with him to fulfill a message which they believed was channeled from God.

This message, as we pay close attention to it, looking through the eyes of modern civilization, can be interpreted as containing fascinating details concerning human social behavior – of women's rights, political changes, transformations within Christianity and everyday life on earth. We find, as we

An angel flies from heaven bearing the Gospel. From the Lincoln College Manuscript – an Anglo-French illuminated manuscript of the Book of Revelation, *c.* 1320 – 30, in the Bodleian Library, Oxford.

Right: The planetary system of Tycho Brahe, based on the Ptolemaic theory, from Andreas Celarius' celestial atlas of the early eighteenth century. At the beginning, astrology and astronomy were one and the same thing. Like most of his contemporaries, the first great astronomer believed firmly in astrology.

Opposite: The vision of St. John. Heaven's door opens at the top of this picture, while the Lamb and the Book are enshrined in the center of a circular Throne. About this centerpiece are the four Beings with the heads of Man, Lion, Ox and Eagle, and the twelve Elders with their symbols of wisdom, here represented by Spanish guitars. From a miniature in the Beatus by Isidoro of Leon, *c.* 1047, at the Biblioteca Nacional in Madrid.

look, that much of what St. John portrayed as our future, matches closely with the predictions of other famous prophets, such as Nostradamus, who wrote long after Jesus had died. During the course of this examination of St. John's Revelation, evidence will be presented to show that John drew upon knowledge of his own pre-Christian, pagan past – of astrological symbolism, of alchemical understanding – and knowledge of the Old Testament writers and prophets such as Daniel.

John was one of the most important of Jesus' disciples. He knew Jesus intimately, lived at his side and listened to everything this extraordinary individual said concerning the way in which mankind could change and improve life on earth. This was a vision for the future, and it is this vision which is encapsulated in the Book of Revelation.

The Vision

CHRISTIANS BELIEVE THAT JOHN WAS VISITED BY AN ANGEL WHO CAME with a message for him from God. We are told that the angel was dressed in a long robe with a golden girdle around the breast, his head and hair as white as snow-white wool, his eyes blazing with fire and his feet shining as brightly as bronze glowing in a furnace. His voice had the sound of water running and there were stars shining out of his right hand. A sharp, two-edged sword came from his mouth and his face was ablaze like the Sun. John is said to have fallen at his feet and the angel told him not to be afraid and then began to relate the contents of the Book of Revelation.

This story is full of drama, power and mythological resonance, and stands as a tribute to Christianity for its ability to inspire faith in the Christian God. And even if we are not inspired by a belief in angels and a god in heaven, we can certainly assume that John received inspiration of some kind from a divine vision.

Revelation was probably physically written largely by John, son of the fisherman Zebedee, who would much later be given the name St. John the Divine. In order to place the writing of the book in context, it is worth taking a brief look at the historical details surrounding that period of John's life.

The Roman historian Suetonius wrote that in around AD 49 some Jews were expelled from Rome for rioting and preaching the word of the new Christian cult. John of Zebedee, one of Jesus' closest disciples, was amongst those expelled.

We can view Christianity at the turn of the first century in our modern calendar as a cult – like many that have been born since that time – attracting as it did the same distrust and disapproval that cults often do today. The Christian cult brought a new belief structure to the Roman Empire and the authorities didn't like it. The Romans pounced on those Jews who attempted to spread the word of Jesus. The disciples of this new religion had a fervency that made them a serious threat to the social cohesion and authority of the Empire. Societies generally don't like new religions, and have a tendency to try to expel or even murder those who propagate them. Jesus' followers were no exception to this treatment, and following their expulsion from Rome some of them traveled to Greece and the island of Patmos to escape further attempts to destroy their new-found faith.

As an exile on this beautiful island off the coast of Asia Minor, John began writing Revelation, which starts with the letters to the seven churches of Asia, in which the Christian doctrine is set out. The letters were written to the churches in the cities of Ephesus, Smyrna, Pergamum, Thyatira, Sardis, Laodicea, and Philadelphia. Almost all interpretations have taken these at little more than their face value – as letters to the churches of the time, written by John, instructing them as to how to behave in a time of religious persecution, but, as we will see later in this book, there may have been a more subtle reason for their writing.

One of the purposes of this book is to attempt to show that these first chapters of the Book of Revelation were written as a kind of map of the progress of humanity, providing step-by-step indicators to the future, as taught to John and the other disciples by Jesus. The balance of the chapters, it is suggested, were intended to provide a more detailed picture of that future. In this case Revelation could be seen as an extraordinary and beautiful rendition of the passion and inspiration of a few men who actually knew Jesus as an inspired teacher and enlightened master.

Orthodox Christianity's early rival in the first century, Gnosticism, embraced the ideals of Greek philosophy and the wisdom of Hinduism, Buddhism and the sacred mystery cults of the Mediterranean. The gnostic gospels, discovered in Nag Hammadi in Egypt in the 1940s, show Jesus in a completely unorthodox light, at least as far as the resulting Christian teaching is concerned — more guru than Messiah during his lifetime.

If we can, so to speak, start again, and try to read the following lines in light of the Gnostic view, we may begin the process of seeing Revelation as something entirely fresh.

The Revelation of Jesus Christ, which God gave unto him, to shew unto his servants things which must shortly come to pass; and he sent and signified it by his angel unto his servant John: Ch. 1:1

These opening lines give us a starting point to work from.

The "revelation" was actually given to John through his divine connection with Jesus – a connection which could well be understood in modern terms, arising from a state of natural awakening or enlightenment. And its purpose was to allow John to show human beings what would come to pass in their future.

Illuminations from the early-fourteenth-century Lincoln College Manuscript.
Top: St. John hears the words of Christ.

Opposite: St. John's vision of the Son of Man. *Above:* An angel casts a millstone into the sea.

Blessed is he that readeth, and they that hear the words of this prophecy, and keep those things which are written therein: for the time is at hand.

¶ John to the seven churches which are in Asia: Grace be unto you, and peace, from his which is, and which was, and which is to come; and from the seven Spirits which are before his throne;

¶ And from Jesus Christ, who is the faithful witness, and the first begotten of the dead, and the prince of the kings of the earth. Unto him that loved us, and washed us from our sins in his own blood,

¶ And hath made us kings and priests unto God and his Father; to him be glory and dominion for ever and ever. Amen.

¶ Behold, he cometh with clouds; and every eye shall see him, and they also which pierced him: and all kindreds of the earth shall wail because of him. Even so, Amen.

¶ I am Alpha and Omega, the beginning and the ending, saith the Lord, which is, and which was, and which is to come, the Almighty.

¶ I John, who also am your brother, and companion in tribulation, and in the kingdom and patience of Jesus Christ, was in the isle that is called Patmos, for the word of God, and for the testimony of Jesus Christ. Ch 1:3-9

Perhaps we can take a closer look at these lines:

And from Jesus Christ, who is the faithful witness, and the first begotten of the dead, and the prince of the kings of the earth.

I John, who also am your brother, and companion in tribulation, and in the kingdom and patience of Jesus Christ, was in the isle that is called Patmos, for the word of God, and for the testimony of Jesus Christ.

In any event, Jesus, perhaps through the presence of an angelic messenger, wanted the existing seven churches to know his message, and instructed John to write to each of them. And in this early part of the text we learn of the vision itself. John tells us:

I was in the Spirit on the Lord's day, and heard behind me a great voice, as of a trumpet,

Saying, I am Alpha and Omega, the first and the last: and, What thou seest, write in a book, and send it unto the seven churches which are in Asia; unto Ephesus, and unto Smyrna, and unto Pergamos, and unto Thyatira, and unto Sardis, and unto Philadelphia, and unto Laodicea.

A detail from the Book of Kells, a
group of manuscripts originating in
Ireland and Britain between the
seventh and tenth centuries AD.
St. Matthew – the Man depicted
as a symbol of the Evangelist.

And then John tells us:

And I turned to see the voice that spake with me. And being turned, I saw seven golden candlesticks…

And in the midst of the seven candlesticks one like unto the Son of man, clothed with a garment down to the foot, and girt about the paps with a golden girdle.

His head and his hairs were white like wool, as white as snow; and his eyes were as a flame of fire;

And his feet like unto fine brass, as if they burned in a furnace; and his voice as the sound of many waters.

And he had in his right hand seven stars: and out of his mouth went a sharp two-edged sword: and his countenance was as the sun shineth in his strength.

And when I saw him, I fell at his feet as dead. And he laid his right hand upon me, saying unto me, Fear not; I am the first and the last:

I am he that liveth, and was dead; and, behold, I am alive for evermore, Amen; and have the keys of hell and of death.

Write the things which thou hast seen, and the things which are, and the things which shall be hereafter;

The mystery of the seven stars which thou sawest in my right hand, and the seven golden candlesticks. The seven stars are the angels of the seven churches: and the seven candlesticks which thou sawest are the seven churches.

Being *in the Spirit on the Lord's day* could have meant literally that John was acting as a priest at the Sabbath service, and while sitting there he heard behind him a great voice – Jesus' voice instructing him to write down in a book what he was told to write. He turned round at this instruction: …*to see the voice that spake with me. And being turned, I saw seven golden candlesticks;*

And in the midst of the seven candlesticks one like unto the Son of man, clothed with a garment down to the foot, and girt about the paps with a golden girdle.

The altar, or holy table, behind where the vision stood, would have had seven candles set out in the style of the early Roman church tradition – three on either side with the seventh in the center, subsequently to symbolize the Pope.

The Book of Revelation, it is therefore suggested, was set down by John following this startling and powerful vision, and as we will perhaps see, it was written as a prophetic study of the future, providing many and varied pictures of the transitions of humanity far into the future beyond John's life.

John of Zebedee was perhaps not sufficiently gifted or knowledgeable to have written Revelation without the help of a divine presence. The text is

Sriaum sancti
cuuangelly seci
dum johanne.

In principio erat
uerbum et ubu
erat apud deum

sophisticated, complex in symbolism and occult knowledge, and full of information regarding matters that would probably not have been privy to a fisherman, however closely he may have been connected with his master, Jesus. As will be suggested during the course of this book, Revelation can be interpreted as being full of astrological, numerological, alchemical, and ancient symbolism, which would only be understood by an individual or individuals broadly educated and aware of much more than the local culture of the time. Such symbolism, and the way it has been mixed in with knowledge of ancient practices from Egypt, Greece and other ancient cultures, would require the mind of a considerable individual. Jesus would certainly have possessed such a mind, and was very likely eminently capable of expressing such complex matters as prophetic, poetic writing in the way that it is seen in Revelation. We may be convinced, therefore, that whatever the nature of the vision presented to John, it could well have provided him with this knowledge.

The scope of the prophecies is wide ranging and multi-faceted. Indeed, the only prophet that we can find in our long history who was as capable and as complex as the writer of Revelation is Nostradamus, who in fact drew on the Bible for much of his symbolism and language.

Revelation was written between the years AD 49-95, during part of which time John was exiled from Rome by the then Roman Emperor, Domitian.

The prophecies form a part of what would become, during medieval history, the vision of a complete synergy in which mankind would grow physically, psychologically, and spiritually into a new world. This new world, as far as the ancient interpreters were concerned, also contained alchemical, astrological and prophetic elements which, when brought together, would provide the individual with an enlightened view of life which essentially would grow into a heaven on earth – a heaven made up of love and self-determination.

From the Christian standpoint, as interpreted by the early Christian "Fathers," those that brought the Christian dogma to the world, everything would come about according to God's law, and this law determined that there would have to be an apocalypse before the "Second Coming" which would then result in a new form of existence. In other words the Messiah would visit earth for a second time and bring with Him the answer to all mankind's problems.

But if we bring a more modern understanding to the subject we may see a much

Opposite: St. John on Patmos contemplating the vision of the Lamb enthroned, the four Beings and the twenty-four Elders. The frontispiece of the illuminated manuscript of the Gospel of St. John in the *Très Riches Heures* of John, Duke of Berry, painted by the Limburg Brothers, 1409-15. In the Musée Condé, Chantilly, France.

Right: Pagan influences permeated early Christian and Jewish art. Mosaic of the zodiac from the sixth-century AD synagogue at Beth Alpha, Israel.

fresher and more human aspect that relies on the individual's capacity to fulfill him or herself. Rather than depending upon some outside entity, and the so-called "end of the world" scenario, perhaps it actually relates more to the internal apocalypse which each individual must encounter before reaching an awakening.

In effect, the fulfilment of Revelation may therefore be the fulfilment of humanity through the self-realization of its individual members. This is not to say that there are not also external aspects to the prophetic nature of Revelation, because whatever happens within the human psyche is also reflected outside it. In effect what we can find, if we look just below the surface of the text, is an incredible picture of a new world that results from human transformation.

Pisces and Aquarius

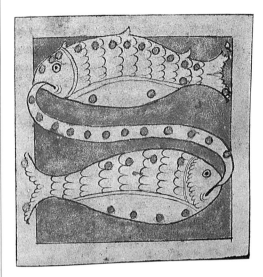

Above: Pisces. *Opposite:* Aquarius. Both from an anonymous twelfth-century treatise on the signs of the zodiac in the Bodleian Library, Oxford.

JUST AS EACH OF US HAS AN ASTROLOGICAL "STAR" SIGN, so, on a grander scale, the movement of the planet earth and all its inhabitants also has a governing sign which changes once every 2000 years or so. We are, in the late twentieth century, at the center of the "change-over" between two different signs – between Pisces and Aquarius. The sign of Pisces has governed planet earth since approximately AD 50, shortly after the crucifixion of Jesus, and around the same time as John was on Patmos composing Revelation. It is no surprise that the dawning of the Age of Pisces and its astrological characteristics coincided with the beginning of Christianity. According to modern interpreters, the Age of Pisces was the age of blind belief, of unquestioned religious faith, of a belief in miracles and magic as the very foundation of life. This naturally gave birth to religious dogma to be obeyed by all – to the idea that the Christian God's existence was unquestioned and that he was the master of all he surveyed.

This belief structure still exists today as a legacy of the past 2000 years, and it is the basis for the majority of people's understanding of Revelation, that God "up there," somewhere in the clouds, makes everything happen.

The concept of the "Second Coming" and the new arrival of the Messiah grew out of the Piscean ideal of external realization – that is, that everything relied upon an otherworldly force which was epitomized by God, who was an all-powerful entity under whom mankind functioned exclusively. During the times of the Piscean Age, which is now coming to an end, humanity was seen as following God and the Church. Because individual volition was subject to His will, the power within each human was believed to be influenced from "above." God was the answer to everything and the Church on earth acted as His director, so to speak, offering guidance and laws which had to be obeyed, for man only knew about himself in relation to God and therefore had less motivation for self-discovery without the aid of the deity. Revelation was therefore seen as a directive from God that would inevitably result in complete global pandemonium, an apocalyptic disaster in which humans, who were essentially sinful (excluding a very few "pure" individuals), would die in the apocalypse and only those who

were pure of heart would survive to people the new world that resulted. The biblical Flood was a precursor of this, bringing water to drown out the sins of mankind and allowing only Noah and his family and animals to return to the dry surface and begin again. Noah was selected by God because of his purity and innocence and the animals were seen as perfect examples of untouched nature, so that this symbolism acted to illustrate the Christian ideal of perfection – the only perfection available on earth.

This biblical purgation myth is echoed in many other cultures – in Native American stories, for example, which tell of a world into which mankind arrived, sinned and then was expelled, leaving the pure of heart to begin again.

The Piscean Age is in its very last stages and we are at the onset of the Aquarian Age, which speaks, through the astrological characteristics of the sign of Aquarius, much more of individual awakening, of the perfection of each human being through a process of spiritual alchemy which turns our individual psyches towards that same heaven, but on earth, through a simple understanding of our natures. The apocalypse would then take place in each of us as we realize the illusions of our lives. The resulting world would be, in fact, a very different place, for the simple reason that when we awaken we see life as it is really meant to be, not as we imagine it should be. There would then, of course, also be a global apocalypse, but as we shall see, it would not be in the manner that we fear it.

The prophetic element of Revelation therefore provides us with a picture which results from this human transformation. The elements of this world, however, are not in any way utopian but contain complex conditions which affect all our surroundings: our politics, our communications, our religious understanding, our relationships, global finances and the general ways in which we operate in our lives.

As we will find in the coming pages, it is possible to weave a tapestry of this new world, that gives us a picture of a way of life which has been glimpsed many times down the ages by the seers and prophets of other religious visions, from ancient Hinduism to some of the modern enlightened masters of the twentieth century. This common vision is based on the prevalence of love as a palpable and existential presence, unrelated to

Below: A Navaho blanket depicting part of their creation myth, with two supernatural "holy people" flanking the sacred maize plant, which was a gift to mortals. They are enclosed in a rainbow arc, the symbol in most religious mythology of the connection between heaven and earth. From the Schindler Collection in New York.

Opposite: Queen Charlotte Islands, British Columbia, Canada. According to Haida legend, these were created when the world was still covered by water. "Raven" created the islands by dropping stones for a resting place, or splashing water and transforming the resulting spray into rock.

Overleaf: Llyn Gwynant, Gwynned, North Wales.

modern, day-to-day concepts of love, but taking the form of a totality arising out of inner silence and enlightenment.

Along the way, before we reach this ideal existence, we must, however, pass through hell, and it is suggested very strongly within the lines of Revelation that this hell is already in full swing during the last years of the twentieth century.

Revelation: The Prophecies – The Apocalypse and Beyond is therefore an outline of an extraordinary, magical treatise on our future which can be seen as perhaps the greatest and most complete work of prophecy in mankind's history, outstripping even the works of the seer Nostradamus. The journey we must take is both fascinating and magical, leading us through a labyrinth of ancient mythology, symbolism and occult understanding to find a treasure of immeasurable value for our future.

CHAPTER

DECODING REVELATION

The Astrology

A S A PRELIMINARY BACKDROP TO THE COMING PROPHECIES, WE CAN TAKE a brief look at some of the astrological symbolism present in the Book of Revelation, if only to give us a sense of one of the methods used to encode the prophetic message of the book. But it should be made clear from the outset that we are using the term astrology in its higher sense, not in the sense of the horoscopes that appear in newspapers and magazines, and assert that one-twelfth of the entire world population will all be behaving in the same way at the same time!

The world-famous astrologer Dane Rudhyar defined this form of astrology in a way that may help us to appreciate its presence in Revelation:

"Astrology, in so far as it is based on astronomical data, deals also with objective time and its cycles. But astrology is not merely a study of celestial cycles in themselves; it is a technique of interpretation of the meaning of these cycles with reference to the possibilities for growth in individuals. …when true to its highest and truest function in human affairs [it] is to indicate the possibilities for individual development inherent in the significant turning points in the cycle of human life…"

After this I looked, and behold, a door was opened in heaven: and the first voice which I heard was as it were of a trumpet talking with me; which said, Come up hither, and I will shew thee things which must be hereafter…

¶ And before the throne there was a sea of glass like unto crystal: and in the midst of the throne, and round about the throne, were four beasts full of eyes before and behind.

¶ And the first beast was like a lion, and the second beast like a calf, and the third beast had a face as a man, and the fourth beast was like a flying eagle.

¶ And the four beasts had each of them six wings about him; and they were full of eyes within: and they rest not day and night, saying, Holy, holy, holy, Lord God Almighty, which was, and is, and is to come. Ch 4 .1-8

Above, top to bottom: Scenes from the Lincoln College Manuscript. The opening of the seventh seal in which the seven angels are given trumpets. The vision of a mighty angel. The army of horsemen bearing plagues. The people of God are told to leave Babylon.

Opposite: The symbols of the four Evangelists from the Book of Kells – St. Matthew (the Man), St. Mark (the Lion), St. Luke (the Calf), and St. John (the Eagle).

The "four beasts" mentioned in Chapter Four of Revelation – the Calf (Ox), the Lion, the Eagle and the Man, relate to the four main zodiacal signs of Taurus, Leo, Scorpio (the eagle), and Aquarius (the human water-bearer). Revelation is not the only book in the Bible where the same four beasts are mentioned. In the

Old Testament Book of Ezekiel, the prophet Ezekiel relates a vision in which scenes appeared to him including a Man, a Lion, an Ox and an Eagle.

The man symbol is accepted throughout astrology as the Water-Bearer of Aquarius, the lion as Leo, the calf or ox obviously indicates the sign of Taurus, and the eagle signifies the higher values of Scorpio, though this is perhaps less well-known except amongst astrologers. The scorpion symbol is the lower psychic expression of the sign of Scorpio, while the eagle is the higher. Manly P. Hall in his book *The Secret Teachings of All Ages,* tells us:

The seven-headed dragon.
Detail from a double-leafed *Beatus*
from eleventh-century Madrid.

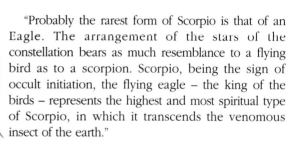

"Probably the rarest form of Scorpio is that of an Eagle. The arrangement of the stars of the constellation bears as much resemblance to a flying bird as to a scorpion. Scorpio, being the sign of occult initiation, the flying eagle – the king of the birds – represents the highest and most spiritual type of Scorpio, in which it transcends the venomous insect of the earth."

It is entirely appropriate that within the Bible the higher forms of astrological symbolism would be used.

These same four symbols appeared also in Egyptian and Babylonian traditions of wisdom, specifically at the entrance to the Great Pyramid of Giza. The archetypical Sphinx is composed of the head of a man, the body of a bull, the claws of a lion and the wings of an eagle. The Bible, as a part of the Christian tradition, integrated these symbols from the distant past and used them to form part of the basis for its prophetic substance. Although astrology is not the primary interpretative force behind Revelation, within the first four chapters we see the scene set by reference to astrological symbols.

Christianity, in fact, attempted to reduce the significance of astrology by emphasizing it's occult, heretical nature. Astrology was concerned with "the heavens," the domain of God, and was therefore forbidden to man, but in the symbology of Revelation it is so clearly present that it has survived through Christianity to remain significant in our interpretations of the predictions. During the course of discovering the "picture" which Revelation draws of the world in our future, we will come across astrological symbols again, each one used by John as a method of explaining his vision.

Opposite: A terracotta mother
goddess from Mohenjodaro in the
Indus Valley, 2300-1750 BC. From
the National Museum of India in
New Delhi.

Symbols of the Pagan

I T COULD BE SAID THAT THOSE WHO TAKE THE BIBLE LITERALLY AS A BASIS for life become somehow hypnotized into a kind of tunnel vision when it comes to discovering its content and meaning. The Bible is the Bible is the Bible – refusing to entertain the idea that there may be much more archaic learning, derived from long before Christianity, that influenced its writing. Obviously the Old Testament, known to have existed hundreds of years before Christ was born, must contain pagan influences. We can accept this perhaps. But to suggest that Revelation might in fact contain, for example, shamanic magic, would seem almost insulting. How could Jesus Christ, or his angel, have been willing to inject such primitive practices into so important a document?

But in fact it could be suggested that Revelation contains much pre-Christian material, much primal magic.

As always with this extraordinary book, the words on the page hide much much more than is at first evident. Take the following lines from Chapter Twelve, for example:

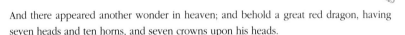

And there appeared another wonder in heaven; and behold a great red dragon, having seven heads and ten horns, and seven crowns upon his heads.

¶ And his tail drew the third part of the stars of heaven, and did cast them to the earth: and the dragon stood before the woman which was ready to be delivered, for to devour her child as soon as it was born.

¶ And she brought forth a man child, who was to rule all nations with a rod of iron: and her child was caught up unto God, and to his throne.

¶ And the woman fled into the wilderness, where she hath a place prepared of God, that they should feed her a thousand two hundred and threescore days.

¶ And there was war in heaven: Michael and his angels fought against the dragon; and the dragon fought and his angels,

¶ And prevailed not; neither was their place found any more in heaven.

¶ And the great dragon was cast out, that old serpent, called the Devil, and Satan, which deceiveth the whole world: he was cast out into the earth, and his angels were cast out with him.

¶ And the serpent cast out of his mouth water as a flood ... Ch. 12:3-15

In his book, *The Way of the Shaman,* Michael Harner tells the story of a visit he made to the Conibo Indians near the Ucayali River region of the Upper Amazon forests in the 1970s. On this essentially anthropological trip he was given a sacred drink made from the vines and leaves of a plant called the cawa. The drink was called the ayahuasca or "soul vine," and was said to have very powerful and dangerous effects on those who took it.

During the extraordinary hallucinations that occurred while under the influence of this primitive, natural shamanistic herb, Harner experienced, having had no previous knowledge of what he saw, the presence of various creatures and scenes that included a massive serpent that gushed water from its mouth, and dragon-like creatures that professed to be intrinsic to the birth of human nature and all life on earth. These dragons were said, in the trance state, to have come to earth following a terrible cosmic battle outside the planet, with forces they could not conquer, being forced to arrive on earth to escape their pursuers.

Harner later visited American evangelist friends and was told that his experience was exactly that described in the Book of Revelation, chapter twelve, in the passage quoted above.

Such ancient knowledge of powers outside human understanding has been the central pivot of shamanic practice for many thousands of years. It is not common only to recent anthropological study, for Harner went on to discover that others had experienced the exact same visions related to dragon-like creatures who once visited humanity.

Whether or not these accounts have any foundation in reality is not relevant, for what we are concerned with is the possibility that their symbolism is evident in the lines of Revelation at a time when shamanic practices were normal in many parts of the world and formed a serious basis for life.

And so the picture of the "subliminal" aspect of Revelation begins to become evident.

We can substantiate the presence of symbols of the ancients, astrology, pagan shamanism and still more – perhaps even numerology.

Astro-Numerics

REVELATION USES NUMBERS THROUGHOUT THE TEXT IN TWO DIFFERENT ways. These numbers carry great significance and work towards giving us a frame of reference for both the dates of the prophecies and as an indication of various other factors in our interpretation.

We can start with one of the "eccentricities" of Revelation, which is that it appears to assign only 360 days to the calendar year. This shortened year is divided up into twelve months of exactly 30 days. There are various places in Revelation where we can find examples of this:

And I will give power unto my two witnesses, and they shall prophesy a thousand two hundred and threescore days... Ch. 11:3

A period of one thousand two hundred and sixty days is also expressed in other parts of the text as forty-two months:

...and the holy city shall they tread under foot forty and two months. Ch. 11:2

We also find the use of the number three and a half:

And they of the people and kindreds and tongues and nations shall see their dead bodies three days and a half... Ch. 11:9

One thousand two hundred and sixty days, or forty two months, or three and a half, all indicate a 360-day year. 1260 divided by 3.5 equals 360 days, 42 months divided by 3.5 equals 12, which is directly divisible into 360.

At the time when John was writing the book, there certainly were not only 360 days in the calendar year, and he would not have been ignorant of the calendar which assigned 365 days to the year, which had been in use in the Middle East for more than a thousand years before his life. For example we find references in the book of Jubilees, which is estimated to have been written around 100 BC, which illustrates the use of the 364-day calendar. The writer S.J. De Vries tells us:

"A purely solar reckoning is employed in the calendar promoted by the

The numerics in Revelation derive from a mixture of ancient knowledge and contemporary sources, reflecting universal prototypes. *Above:* Mayan calendar with numerals and a center scene of an altar with two priests, skulls and bones. From Tikal, Guatemala, AD 500-900.
Opposite: A modern copy of an Aztec calendar.

Side by side stand a stone *Menorah* of the Second Temple period with an eighteenth-century version made from solid silver. Each branch of the candelabrum stands for a day in Chanukah, the Jewish feast of lights. The numerical value of these ancient symbols has potent mystical significance.

sectarian book of Jubilees (circa 105 BC). Throughout this remarkable book a year of 364 days is prescribed..."

F. Aster Barnwell suggests, in his book *Meditations on the Apocalypse*, that it is more likely that John used this exact system not as actual calendar days and months but as a metaphor for the astrological zodiacal wheel, which contains 360 degrees and is divided up into twelve signs of 30 degrees each.

What John was perhaps in effect doing, therefore, was providing us with a link between time and the astrological method of measuring it. As Aster Barnwell continues to tell us:

"When the year and the zodiacal wheel are made to coincide, units of time such as years, months, and days become equivalent to zodiacal revolutions, signs, and degrees respectively. This means that references to events that are hinged upon a specific duration of time can be interpreted in terms of spatial concepts, i.e. degrees of the zodiac."

This representation of time and the astrological zodiac as being the same has been around for thousands of years. It serves to keep the text available for any future date or any race or creed, for the calendar is no longer needed. Calendars change, the planets and their movement do not. John thus provided a secure method of projecting his prophecies into the future.

It is suggested also that the other method that can be used to interpret the text of Revelation is the Gematria, the Hebrew numeric system that turns numbers into words and vice versa. The Gematria provides us with some fascinating proposals, and we have used this method to understand the famous number 666, supposedly the "number of the beast" or Satan, whereas in fact it may symbolize something much more exciting and enigmatic than a simple devil, as we shall see later.

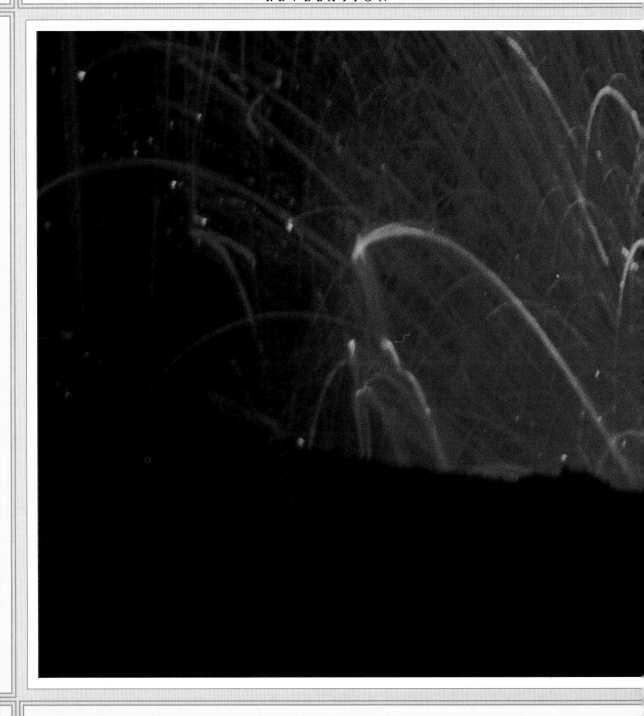

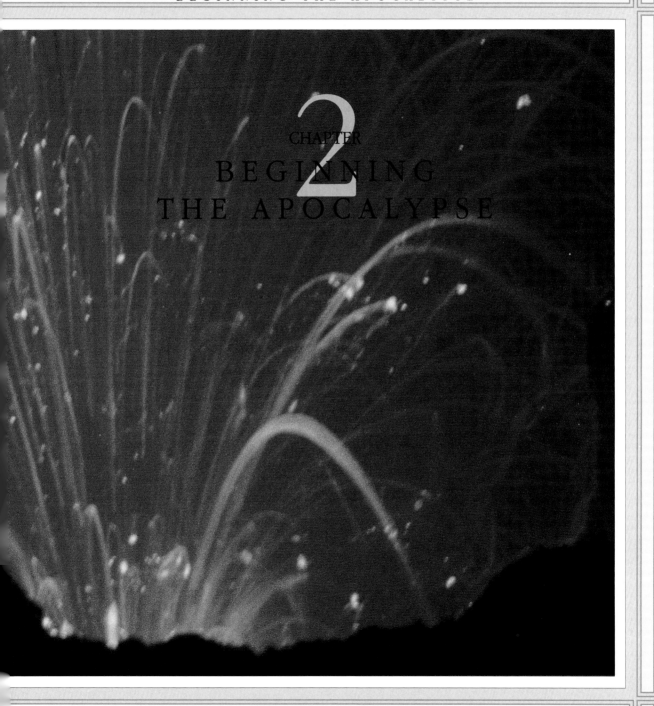

CHAPTER

2

BEGINNING THE APOCALYPSE

The Seven Ages of Man

Above: A medieval view of man's place in the Creation. Miniature from the German saint and mystic Hildegard of Bingen's *Liber Divinorum Operum.*
Opposite: St. Michael and his angels fight with the dragon.

Previous pages: Volcanic eruption in Vanuatu, in the southwestern Pacific Ocean.

THE FIRST PART OF JOHN'S TEXT BEGINS WITH LETTERS TO seven cities in Asia. These letters were written, as we have already mentioned, to the churches of the cities of Ephesus, Smyrna, Pergamum, Thyatira, Sardis, Laodicea, and Philadelphia, and many interpreters have simply accepted them on face value.

There is, however, perhaps a more exciting way of looking at these short pieces – a way that was partly suggested by Rudolf Steiner in his book *The Apocalypse of St. John,* and further explained by F. Aster Barnwell in his book *Meditations on the Apocalypse,* the proposals of which we shall now look at in greater detail. For it can be interpreted, as we shall see, that these seven letters outline the spiritual evolution of human life on earth. Understanding this possible interpretation of the use of the seven cities of Asia by John, may help us to put the rest of Revelation in a prophetic context. First we need, however, to establish some sense of whether these seven letters were included in Revelation for other reasons.

The seven cities in Revelation probably were not chosen simply for their religious or geographic significance. Classical geographers used the name Asia in two different senses. First, it referred to the present-day continent, and second, it also described the province opposite Europe on the Dardanelles Straits – the western third of modern Turkey. The provincial use is the origin of our term Asia Minor, as opposed to the continental use, Asia Major. The word "city" was also used in a different sense in those times. It meant something similar to a county and referred to the whole district in which the urban center was located. The province of Asia contained some one hundred and fifty cities altogether, and these seven cities happen to be located close to where Revelation was, it is believed, largely written, on the island of Patmos.

Pergamum, Ephesus and Smyrna were certainly the most important three cities in the province, from the point of view of their influence and size, and it is quite possible that Sardis and Laodicea ranked fourth and fifth in size and importance. But the remaining two cities cannot have been included because of their size: Cyzicus was certainly a more important place than either Philadelphia or Thyatira, and we know, from an inscription on a coin of the Roman Emperor

An eighteenth-century mystical diagram from *The Imperial Standard of Messiah Triumphant* by Richard Roach, published in London in 1727. The numbers one to seven beneath the circles denote the seven churches of Asia. The Roman numerals above the circles express the various stages of Christ's process from his birth to his emergence in glory at the end of the world, and then return again to the beginning, symbolizing the "Alpha and Omega" of spiritual growth. The British Library, London.

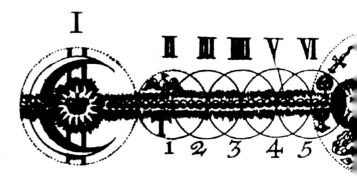

Gordian III, that the seventh most important city was Magnesia. So size was not the determining factor.

Nor can the list be a matter of the precedence of the Christian Churches, because the Church at Colossae, near Laodicea, was older and more important, going back a generation to the days of St. Paul.

So the purpose of these letters probably wasn't related to the importance or size of the cities which they addressed, and in fact, putting them against the rest of Revelation, there might not seem to be any reason for having the letters at all, unless they contain some deeper significance.

Instead, let us consider the possibility that the letters to the churches of Asia outline an extremely subtle form of human evolution that we are experiencing.

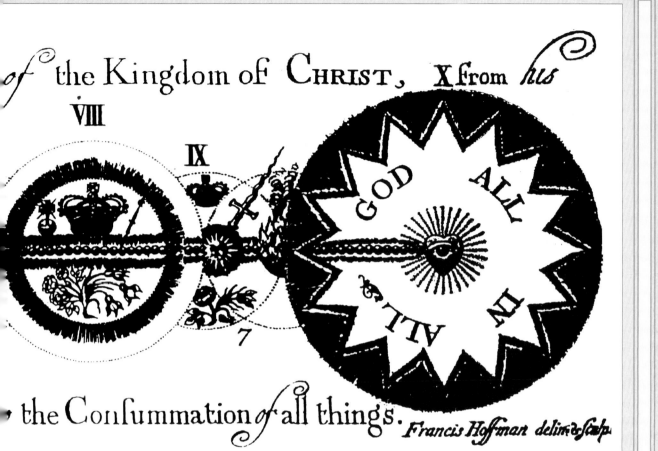

of the Kingdom of CHRIST, X from his

the Consummation of all things.

Francis Hoffman delin & sculp.

Opposite: The seven cities of Asia
(Anatolia), whose Christian
communities St. John addresses
in his letters. In the first and
second centuries, the province of
Asia was the wealthiest part of
the Roman Empire.

This particular manifestation of human evolution could be
expressed as an evolution of the soul, if we regard the soul as
the source of motivation for our broader changes – or put
another way, the motivation for the changes that take place over
many lifetimes.

The concept of the soul's existence beyond one physical life
emerges from at least four of the main organized religions.
Within Buddhism, Hinduism and Jainism there is a confirmed positive belief,
which forms part of the structure of the religion in each case, that the soul
inhabits many bodies through many lifetimes. Within Christianity there is a
confirmed negative belief in relation to reincarnation of the soul, but a positive
belief that the soul somehow passes from the body after one life and resides
either in heaven or in hell. Christianity, therefore, supports the concept of a
soul, but only accords it one physical manifestation, allotting its further
processes to either joy or terror.

But it is the contention of this chapter that, manifested within the seven letters
to the seven churches of Asia, John's message from God was in fact concerned
with a spiritual evolution of the soul, whether it be over a single life or many
hundreds or thousands of lives. The number seven, as we have discussed, is
generally accepted by most magical, pagan or religious traditions as symbolic.

In order to establish some reference points for this theory about the seven
letters in Revelation, we must now look for evidence from our past for the
possible existence of a spiritual evolution in humanity, an evolution that may be
seen to have seven stages to it.

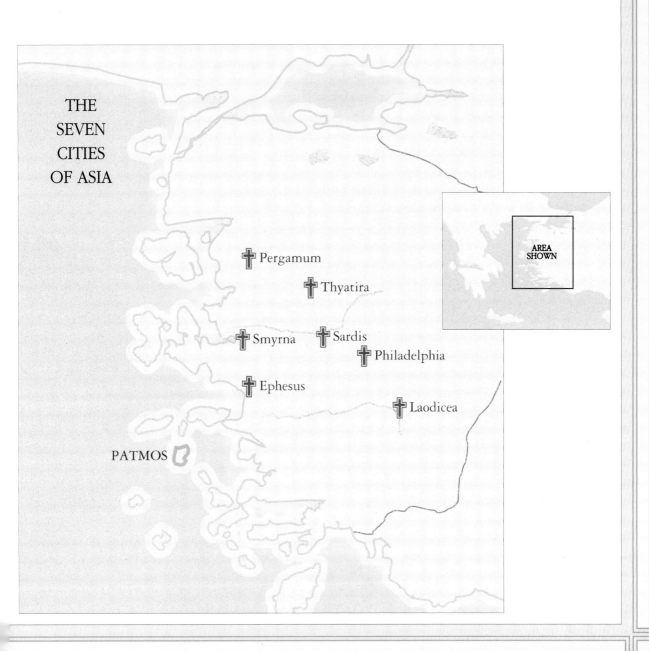

THE
SEVEN
CITIES
OF ASIA

AREA
SHOWN

✝ Pergamum

✝ Thyatira

✝ Smyrna   ✝ Sardis

✝ Philadelphia

✝ Ephesus

✝ Laodicea

PATMOS

The Perennial Philosophy

I N THE MYSTICS' WORLD OF THE EAST, THERE ARE A NUMBER OF WHAT WE might term "maps," which were originally constructed to give spiritual seekers some sense of direction on the complex path to the awakening consciousness. These maps occur in ancient Eastern and Western disciplines such as Tao, Gnosticism, Sufism, Zen, and Hinduism, and although there are differences in detail, the major aspects are, extraordinarily, the same. Aldous Huxley, the twentieth-century novelist and philosopher, was fascinated by the teachings of the various eastern mystics. He undertook to explain some aspects of the religious ideas of, for example, India, where thought and proof – "referenced certainty" – are not the norm. The religious disciple of the "East" accepts the word of his Master, without need for proof, because the very basis for his education results in a better contact with his instinctual nature rather than his mentality. Those that originated these maps did not "theorize" about the concepts they offered, they "knew." From first-hand experience, the seers and mystics of our past and present create such cosmologies out of lifetimes of esoteric experience (that is, an experience of the inner consciousness). The West has chosen to explore the exoteric realm – the external phenomena of life – as opposed to the esoteric realm, which looks inwards and therefore has a greater connection with those deeper instincts that Western man has largely lost touch with.

The resulting reliance upon the "proven" word makes the understanding of something as subtle as Revelation extremely difficult, as we are traveling into realms that have no proven background, and require the individual to get in better touch with the esoteric, or inner boundaries of his or her being.

But, for the purpose of attempting to translate the untranslatable for the Western mind, we can use the method undertaken by Huxley.

Huxley adopted a term used by the German philosopher Leibnitz – *Philosophia Perennis* or the Perennial Philosophy – defining it as "the ethic that places man's final end in the knowledge of the immanent *(intrinsic)* and transcendental Ground of all Being." Put another way, this map is an abiding philosophy which survives all seasons and changes of era. The concept derives from a number of eminent sources, including the Hindu Vedanta, Christian Gnosticism, Mahayana Buddhism and the Christian concept of the "Kenosis," which outlines levels of spiritual evolution. According to the Vedanta, which

Mankind as a spiritually evolving species. These diagrams interpret two aspects of *evolution* and *involution,* according to the teacher Meher Baba. The original void at the top of the inverted S "evolves" through seven stages culminating in God in the consciousness of man. That

consciousness then proceeds to "involve" through a further seven stages returning to the original void transformed. The dual processes are intertwined in one whole like an inward and outward breath.

forms the very basis of Hindu religious understanding, the seven levels of spiritual evolution form part of "The Great Chain of Being" – a kind of progress system that all humanity must undertake to reach perfection or enlightenment.

So, to start our reference for the seven levels of human evolution, we can assume that this map of spiritual growth has been around in the philosophies and ideas of human religiousness for thousands of years unchanged. It is a perennial idea, and does not alter through the fashions of human understanding.

Western science, for example, can adopt only theories which must inevitably change and need updating with the arrival of new evidence. Even the great theories of scientists such as Newton and Einstein have not withstood the progress of time, whereas the mystical counterparts of these men, people such as Jesus, Mahavira, Buddha, used no such devices. A blind man has a theory about how the sun rises, while a man with his eyes open needs no theory, for he has seen the sun rise. The problem for the mystic is the translation of this direct and overwhelming experience into words which mean something to the blind man. The blind man cannot trust the mystic – one of the reasons why "gurus" and mystics from the East have so much trouble in the West is that the Western mind does not know trust. Trust, in this sense, does not mean unquestioned faith as in the Christian understanding, for trust, as understood within the Eastern religious philosophies, is still capable of questioning and doubt.

So the most important and first principle of the Perennial Philosophy is that of hierarchy. There are stages, or planes, or levels of growth to awakening. These levels, however, are not one upon the other, piled up like a stack of books, each one higher than the last. They are more like nesting dolls, each one unscrewing to reveal another inside it. Each ascending level includes all the levels below it, so an understanding on level one would be included in the living organism of level two. But it does not work the other way about. The understanding does not contain the living organism. Put another way, the more highly evolved organism includes the less evolved, but the less evolved does not contain the higher.

The essential theme of all scriptures then, can be encapsulated in these "levels" of attainment to the ideal. For the sake of simplicity we will attempt to provide them in a suitably Western form, though even expressed in this way the following is already difficult to encompass with the understanding of the relatively unsophisticated device of thought:

1. PHYSICAL MATTER – where the interest lies in purely physical activities and concepts – such as a small child's concern with understanding and learning about his/her own body. This is before there becomes any awareness of consciousness, psychology or even biology. No disillusionment has yet taken place. There is still belief in the obvious, in the external.

2. BIOLOGY – where the interest turns inwards for the first time and the individual encounters self-reflection.

3. THE REALM OF PSYCHOLOGY AND THOUGHT – the place where the vast majority of humanity now resides, where everything is based on thought and the mind is believed to be the supreme device. But there are already many individuals who know this is not the case, for the moment thought is abandoned, something more exciting and powerful appears.

4. THE PSYCHIC HEART – where instinct and "knowing" replace the past-conscious workings of the mind. Here the individual discovers power and energy through freedom from a purely intellectual state.

5. THE SUBTLE PLANE – the fear of death disappears at this level and the individual experiences a closer connection with "the whole," or "oneness" with existence.

6. THE CAUSAL LEVEL – this is the level where a formless radiance occurs and the individual approaches enlightenment. It could also be called the first level of "realization." Masters and mystics such as Jesus and Lao Tzu could be seen as being on this level.

7. ONENESS – here the individual has risen to a final awakening and all experience disappears and is replaced with primal consciousness. In effect the individual dies to all existential behavior and merges with the whole of existence.

Humanity as a whole, then, probably exists in greater part at level three, the realm of thought.

Given our attempt at "referenced certainty," and the discussion in the previous section which indicated the common presence of the number seven as a mystical indicator, we can begin to look at the seven letters to the Churches of Asia in this light, and see perhaps how John intended to use the Perennial Philosophy of the Vedanta as a basis for the letters to the churches in Asia. We can try to get a more detailed understanding of the different levels that we, as individuals, and the world as a whole, may face in the future.

These letters may also form the foundation, along with other aspects of the text, of the picture we are going to paint of our future.

We begin with the letter to Ephesus.

Opposite: The seven levels of spiritual evolution are often represented as a sort of nesting doll with one-way mirrors so that the individual who looks up at the level above sees only his own being reflected in a mirror, while those who inhabit the higher levels can always look down clearly at the levels below them.

Physical Matter

Biology

Psychology and Thought

Psychic Heart

Subtle Plane

Causal Level

Oneness

1. Ephesus

Unto the angel of the church of Ephesus write; These things saith he that holdeth the seven stars in his right hand, who walketh in the midst of the seven golden candlesticks;

¶ I know thy works, and thy labour, and thy patience, and how thou canst not bear them which are evil: and thou hast tried them which say they are apostles, and are not, and hast found them liars:

¶ And hast borne, and hast patience, and for my name's sake hast laboured, and hast not fainted.

¶ Nevertheless I have somewhat against thee, because thou hast left thy first love....

¶ He that hath an ear, let him hear what the Spirit saith unto the churches; To him that overcometh will I give to eat of the tree of life, which is in the midst of the paradise of God. Ch. 2:1-7

Illuminations from the twelfth-century astrological treatise in the Bodleian Library. *Top,* Capricorn, and *above,* Cancer.
Opposite: Artemis, goddess of the Ephesians. A marble statue, *c.* AD 135-175, from the Ephesus Museum in Turkey. The Temple of Artemis at Ephesus was the first in antiquity to be built entirely of marble.

THE FIRST KEY WORDS IN THIS LETTER ARE: *and thou hast tried them which say they are apostles, and are not, and hast found them liars:*
Emphasis is on the attempt to believe – *thou hast tried them which say they are apostles.* A failure to believe has occurred – *and hast found them liars.* Disillusionment has occurred. The first level of the physical still applies, but disillusionment follows. The body of evidence no longer has sway over the individual.

John's message then continues to emphasize the need for perseverance – *And hast borne, and hast patience, and for my name's sake hast laboured, and hast not fainted. And gently chastises us – Nevertheless I have somewhat against thee, because thou hast left thy first love....*

The first love is the physical – the child revels in the body, learning and touching and feeling, even experiencing innocent sensuous energy. This was our first love and we should not leave it behind too simply.

Seen on a global scale, the message then in this first letter could be seen to be that mankind must undergo a period of disillusionment. The concept, for example, of the old Christianity (the Piscean ideal) which has held sway for so many centuries – that there is an external God – will perhaps lose many

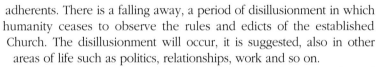

adherents. There is a falling away, a period of disillusionment in which humanity ceases to observe the rules and edicts of the established Church. The disillusionment will occur, it is suggested, also in other areas of life such as politics, relationships, work and so on.

The predominant astrological symbolism in this verse is derived from the connections of Ephesus with the goddess Artemis, whose presence dominated the city, the temple of Artemis being regarded as one of the seven wonders of the world of the time. Artemis represented the Great Mother and her astrological sign was Cancer, which is ruled astrologically by the Moon.

Her main "personal" symbol was that of the bee, which gives us the other side of the astrological polarity – that of Capricorn. In his book *Man and His Gods: Encyclopedia of the World's Religions,* Geoffrey Parrinder refers to her as follows:

"Artemis of Ephesus, the Mother Goddess shown with many breasts – some scholars have interpreted them as the ova of the sacred bee which can be seen adorning the figure."

Mention of the: *seven stars in his right hand, who walketh in the midst of the seven golden candlesticks,* refers, it is suggested, to the Capricornian ability to enter into the matters of the mind, rational understanding and mastery over the principles of life represented by the seven stars. Capricorn is the sign of ambition and comprehension – climbing the mountain of knowledge like the goat, always going upwards to the top.

In making this journey mankind has learned to forget the magic of the more subtle mysteries, through a need to concentrate on the physical level of existence, and thereby denies its spiritual being in favor of ambition and success.

In the last lines we are told: *He that hath an ear, let him hear what the Spirit saith unto the churches; To him that overcometh will I give to eat of the tree of life, which is in the midst of the paradise of God.*

Put very simply, John tells us that we can still listen to the word of God – *let him hear what the Spirit saith unto the churches* – that the message of spirituality still remains intact despite the ambition of Capricornian efforts towards economics and order and the rationality of science and technology.

This period of disillusion might well be seen by humanity as a positive aspect of our present and future. As more individuals become disillusioned by the teachings of past generations – in religion, politics, economy, marriage and so on – so new methods will be discovered and encouraged, and life will change for the better. An example might be the important changes in women's rights that have grown out of feminism, which we might suggest grew out of female disillusionment with past attitudes.

Opposite and above: The elegant Roman vaults and arches of the Temple of Hadrian in Ephesus. The prosperous cities of Anatolia rivaled Rome itself in comfort and beauty.

2. Smyrna

Top, St. John preaching to the seven churches in Asia, and *above,* writing the seven letters. From the Lincoln College Manuscript.
Opposite: A representation of the sign of Virgo, from a sixteenth-century celestial globe in the Science Museum, London.

And unto the angel of the church in Smyrna write; These things saith the first and the last, which was dead, and is alive;

¶ I know thy works, and tribulation, and poverty, (but thou art rich) and I know the blasphemy of them which say they are Jews, and are not, but are the synagogue of Satan.

¶ Fear none of those things which thou shalt suffer: behold, the devil shall cast some of you into prison, that ye may be tried; and ye shall have tribulation ten days: be thou faithful unto death, and I will give thee a crown of life.

¶ He that hath an ear, let him hear what the Spirit saith unto the churches; He that overcometh shall not be hurt of the second death. Ch. 2:8-11

THE CITY OF SMYRNA DATES BACK TO MORE THAN A THOUSAND YEARS before Christ when it was founded as an Aeolian Greek colony which was then captured by Ionian Greeks. Around 600 BC it was destroyed by the Lydians and then rebuilt from a design given by Alexander the Great to the Macedonian general Lysimachus, from a dream that Alexander had had in which the goddess of Smyrna, Nemesis, gave the full plan of the new city to him.

Stage two in the seven levels of evolutionary change, if we remember, is that of "biology" – the first step towards the inner search, moving from the purely unaware physical first stage towards introspection. And the second letter exemplifies this change towards self-reflection.

The first hint we get from the letter to Smyrna lies in the first line:

These things saith the first and the last, which was dead, and is alive;

In Eastern mystical terms, the death by disillusionment is followed by the birth of a new realization. The physical stage dies to the more introspective "biological," and the individual becomes self-aware, a "turning-in" – something totally familiar to those who have walked the path of religious and spiritual development. John's words can be interpreted as meaning therefore that the human spirit could undergo this process as a critical mass of disillusioned individuals is reached. Humanity would thereby take a new interest in those things that were supposedly long dead.

He goes on to make the point still clearer:

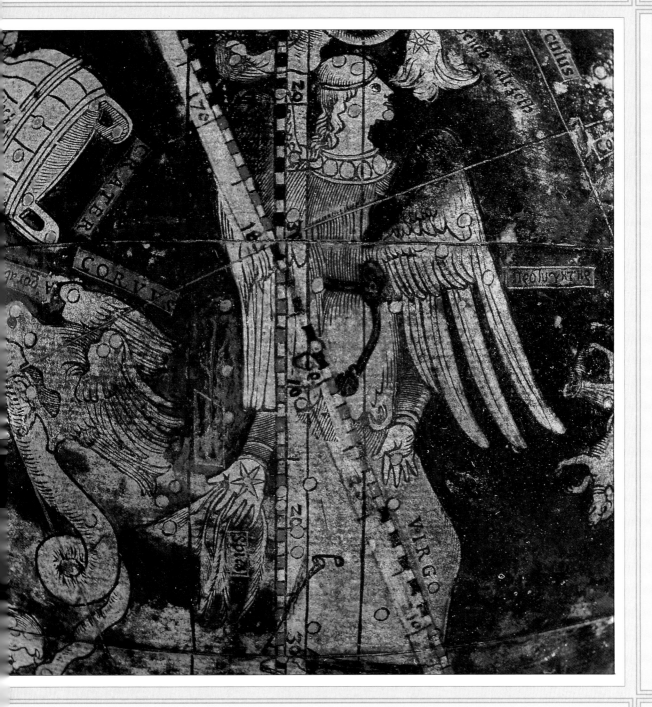

I know thy works, and tribulation, and poverty, (but thou art rich)…

The disillusionment leads to a poverty of appreciation – a kind of boredom with life as it has been – but still the human spirit is rich enough to find new ways.

And finally he gives hope to those who may find change a problem, with a kind of confidence-boosting word:

Fear none of those things which thou shalt suffer: behold, the devil shall cast some of you into prison, that ye may be tried; and ye shall have tribulation ten days: be thou faithful unto death, and I will give thee a crown of life.

The astrological characteristic of the Smyrna letter derives from the city's adherence to the goddess Nemesis, who appeared as twin figures, and was therefore associated with the twin Pisces sign.

In his book *Helen of Troy – Woman and Goddess,* Jack Lindsay writes:

"Especially in later phases the [Nemesis] cult showed a strong syncretizing trend; Nemesis took over the attribution of others, most of all in Smyrna and Alexandria, and the conflation with Fate and Fortune gave her the Wheel of the City – Tyche."

The characteristics of the goddess Nemesis in her double form of Fate and Fortune seem most closely to associate with the astrological characteristics of the Virgo-Pisces polarity – Virgo being the process that is born out of the death of one life and the birth of another when Capricornian ambition and rationality has turned towards self-discovery. Virgo also epitomizes the physical conditions of life, that is the body, health and work to sustain the body. Pisces is further associated with the unconscious. Once the individual, for example, abandons work which is done simply for financial gain there might be the opportunity to find new pastures through greater self-reflection. Virgo's characteristics are those of a verification process, consciously dealing with an accumulation of experience in order to find one's outer limits – forming a picture of oneself. "Virgo energy asserts itself in one's consciousness when one stops taking things for granted." (F.Aster Barnwell – *Meditations on the Apocalypse*)

On the other side of the astrological character coin, there is the presence of the symbolism of Pisces. Virgo self-reflection creates a sense of unease and hesitancy. The process of self-reflection alone tends perhaps to make the individual more hesitant, and therefore less able to make the decisions needed to function in normal social and work situations – to conclude the "sales" of life. The sign of Pisces, the two fish intertwined – the first and the last – brings the unification of both ends of the human principle: verification by self-discovery and confirmation by acceptance of the self.

One of the main features of the stage of evolution outlined by the letter to Smyrna is a questioning of established religious dogma. Today, alternative or fringe

religions are a common sight in any major city throughout the world. *Above:* The twenty-fifth birthday celebration of the Hare Krishna group in London.

The message we may find, then, by interpreting this verse of Revelation in this way, is perhaps that we must utilize both sides of the coin in our search for the new way – and be unified within ourselves. Dropping-out of society is no use to anyone, let alone the drop-out. We may perhaps do better by accepting our natures and the nature of our "home" environment. Acceptance creates joy, creates usefulness.

3. Pergamum

And to the angel of the church in Pergamos write; These things saith he which hath the sharp sword with two edges; ....

¶ But I have a few things against thee, because thou hast there them that hold the doctrine of Balaam, who taught Balac to cast a stumbling block before the children of Israel, to eat things sacrificed unto idols, and to commit fornication.

¶ So hast thou also them that hold the doctrine of the Nicolaitans, which thing I hate.

¶ Repent; or else I will come unto thee quickly, and will fight against them with the sword of my mouth.

¶ He that hath an ear, let him hear what the Spirit saith unto the churches; To him that overcometh will I give to eat of the hidden manna, and will give him a white stone, and in the stone a new name written, which no man knoweth saving he that receiveth it. Ch. 2:12-17

The letter to the church in Pergamum was perhaps intended to indicate the stage in our development that brings us to understanding communication on a deeper level than the mind – communication from heart to heart – without prejudices, and without mistrust.

Above: The signs of Gemini and Sagittarius, from the twelfth-century Bodleian manuscript.

Opposite: Scene at an anti-Nazi rally, Brick Lane, London, 1993.

THE LETTER TO PERGAMUM CAN BE INTERPRETED AS TAKING US INTO THE next stage, a stage that humanity is currently involved in – stage three in our seven levels of consciousness – that of thought as the most prevalent form of understanding.

These things saith he which hath the sharp sword with two edges...

This image of the two-edged sword is a commonly used device to indicate that on the one side there may be power in having such a weapon in our hands – the weapon of the intellect and its capability to attack problems and solve them through mental activity – but on the other side there are the problems that arise from too much reliance on intellect and not enough upon instinct, upon the heart. In the description that John gives of his first sight of the angel that visits him, he speaks of a sword issuing from the mouth. This symbolizes the mouth of communication and psychological consciousness, a consciousness that is capable of cutting through illusions and falsehoods – the raised consciousness which has reached a state of understanding through the intellect.

We may see the less positive side of the intellectual two-edged sword in the predominance of distrust because of too great an adherence to thought as a method of judging ourselves and others. Fighting always with the sword of one's mouth brings stress and constant analysis – every question brings another question.

The astrological symbolism of this stage of John's prophetic message would seem to be derived from Pergamum's constant central interest in education, reasoning and religious faith, thus giving us the polarity of Gemini and Sagittarius. The presiding deity at Pergamum was Athene, who was venerated as goddess of the arts and prudent intelligence.

Essentially this would appear to be about releasing ourselves from the process of self-analysis and moving into concern for others.

Thus we can perhaps see the process unfold, for in this evolutionary growth humanity needs to move from the physical body and the sciences of the physical mind – Capricorn – through turning in and examining our inner selves – Virgo and Pisces – to an understanding of the power to change reality and achieve power by letting go of the mind as a primary force – Gemini and Sagittarius.

The letter refers to the biblical story of Balaam and Balak. In this parable a diviner named Balaam was called upon by Balak, King of Moab, to put a curse on the Children of Israel while they remained camped in the land of Moab on their way to the Promised Land (Numbers 22-24). Balak wished to get rid of these people and expected Balaam to use his considerable psychic powers to help him.

It could therefore be interpreted that we are being told that when humanity reaches a position where it has the powers of Balaam, it has at that stage begun to rely less upon the simplicity of psychology and the mind, and must beware not to use the untried powers of psychic instincts against others to manipulate situations and cause suffering as a result.

This is a simple warning. When we have achieved the power to create our own reality. Whether it be political or economic power, we must use it wisely. We are instructed not *to eat things sacrificed unto idols, and to commit fornication.*

It is suggested that this reference in biblical terms does not mean that we should not have pre-marital sex. It is likely that the natural processes of human sexual relationships are not concerned with rigid rules of behavior – God probably doesn't worry about a wedding band. The phrase not "to commit fornication" more likely refers to not making liaisons for pure expediency, but to making relationships all over the world in a way that is concerned for the best – communicating from the heart instead of the mind.

Opposite: The goddess Pallas Athene, by Gustav Klimt. Athena, the virgin warrior, embodied lucid intelligence – a quality vital both for war and for the development of culture.

4. Thyatira

Above: The constellations of Aries and Libra on the celestial globe in the Science Museum, London.
Opposite: The harlot in Revelation shown drunk with the blood of the saints, from the Lincoln College Manuscript.

And unto the angel of the church in Thyatira write; These things saith the Son of God who hath his eyes like unto a flame of fire, and his feet are like fine brass;

¶ I know thy works, and charity, and service, and faith, and thy patience, and thy works; and the last to be more than the first.

¶ Notwithstanding I have a few things against thee, because thou sufferest that woman Jezebel, which calleth herself a prophetess, to teach and to seduce my servants to commit fornication, and to eat things sacrificed unto idols.

¶ And I gave her space to repent of her fornication; and she repented not.

¶ Behold, I will cast her into a bed, and them that commit adultery with her into great tribulation, except they repent of their deeds.

¶ And I will kill her children with death; and all the churches shall know that I am he which searcheth the reins and hearts: and I will give unto every one of you according to your works.

¶ But unto you I say, and unto the rest in Thyatira, as many as have not this doctrine, and which have not known the depths of Satan, as they speak; I will put upon you none other burden.

¶ But that which ye have already hold fast till I come.

¶ And he that overcometh, and keepeth my works unto the end, to him will I give power over the nations:

¶ And he shall rule them with a rod of iron; as the vessels of a potter shall they be broken to shivers: even as I received of my Father.

¶ And I will give him the morning star.

¶ He that hath an ear, let him hear what the Spirit saith unto the churches. Ch. 2:18-29

THE CITY OF THYATIRA WAS FOUNDED AS A MILITARY OUTPOST BY THE Macedonian general Seleucus Nicator (358?-280 BC) who founded the Seleucid dynasty in the struggles that followed the death of Alexander the Great. His empire was centered on Syria and Iran. The city lay in the mouth of a long valley that functioned as a natural communication route for the Macedonians and then later for Rome itself. There were no natural fortifications such as hills or water, so the city relied heavily for its preservation on the strength and courage of its soldiers. Thyatira was known, therefore, as a city constantly ready for combat – a city of

power. And here we find the first connection with the fourth stage of our evolutionary journey – "the psychic heart" – where instinct and "knowing" replace the past-conscious workings of the mind. Here the individual discovers power and energy through freedom from a purely intellectual state.

It is suggested that the astrological signs related to the city of Thyatira can be deduced from the pagan deities that were most actively worshipped there at the time, namely the divine smith Hephaestus and the goddess Pallas Athene – Mars and Venus being their ruling planets, with the astrological signs Aries (Mars) and Libra (Venus) as polar and gender opposites. In purely astrological terms this combination might be interpreted as a particularly representative allegory of what John was proposing in the letter to Thyatira, insofar as Hephaestus and Pallas Athene did not represent a pure male/female archetypical polarity within the Greek and Roman traditions, but served as psychological and biological principles at a stage where transformation had already begun. Put another way, these were gods that were seen to have passed beyond the original forms they had adopted.

Above: The English visionary
William Blake's color-printed
engraving of enlightened man
entitled **Glad Day,** *c.* 1795.
Opposite: Industry has used women
as devices for selling – a trend that
has recently come in quite rightly
for a lot of criticism.

Gods and goddesses in Rome, for example, often underwent changes in their character and in the powers that were ascribed to them. Mars, for example, only became god of war when Rome adopted him, transforming him from his original pagan concern with agriculture. Hephaestus and Pallas Athene were perhaps used by John in Revelation as allegories for this process of transformation. Athena, astrologically epitomized by the sign of Libra, characterized peace-making, while Hephaestus, astrologically epitomized by Aries and the old form of Mars, embodied a concern for land and development. This relationship can be seen as one of transformation from war and conflict into peace and concern for natural development.

These things saith the Son of God who hath his eyes like unto a flame of fire, and his feet are like fine brass…

The *eyes like a flame of fire* of this "Son of God" are eyes that see clearly and reflect the connections between the outside and the inside, making peace within after the conflicts of the mind have been resolved. Anyone who has visited the Eastern world of the various masters who have lived in this century, will have seen eyes that flame like fire, for the enlightenment of human nature produces, literally, a flame-like quality in the eyes. *…feet like fine brass* are feet that stand firmly, well rooted to the ground, giving stability and strength. This is John's description of humanity at the fourth stage of evolutionary consciousness.

Other parts of this short prophetic text contain warnings, as in the other letters. The author uses the same device that was used in the Pergamum letter when he told the story of Balaam. This time it is the now infamous Jezebel, Phoenician Queen of Ahab, King of Israel. In the twentieth century she has become an evangelistic byword for sinful behavior. Her name is evoked to "smite" sinful individuals with expectations of disaster. Much of the modern "fire and damnation" scenarios of various churches in the United States derive from the misuse of phrases and names from Revelation.

On the surface, what is said in this part of Revelation would seem to be a perfect justification for the suppression of certain female characteristics, and in fact this, and similar sentiments from other biblical sources, would probably have provided those in power within State and Church in the past centuries with ample opportunity for burning witches at the stake.

The use of Jezebel as a symbol could perhaps be better interpreted to mean the temporal, superficial joys and doubtful truths of life – such as short-term gains – as opposed to the more laudable characteristics that are suggested by the presence of the gods Hephaestus and Athena who represent peace-making and stability. John indicates that the "children" of

Jezebel – the consequences of short-sighted life choices – will die "from death;" that is, become redundant quickly through lack of energy. This chastisement might therefore be interpreted as meaning that humanity is best advised to adopt the characteristics of the resident gods of Thyatira, in being total in everything we do, and to make our choices only from the best and long-lasting.

Thus the offspring of Jezebel could indicate our false hopes and muddled attitudes to life – poor consciousness, which will pass at the fourth stage of human evolution.

5. *Sardis*

Opposite: Leo, from the twelfth-century Bodleian manuscript.
Above: The signs of Leo and Aquarius, from the Science Museum, London.

And unto the angel of the church in Sardis write; These things saith he that hath the seven Spirits of God, and the seven stars; I know thy works, that thou hast a name that thou livest, and art dead....

¶ Remember therefore how thou hast received and heard, and hold fast, and repent. If therefore thou shalt not watch, I will come on thee as a thief, and thou shalt not know what hour I will come upon thee.

¶ Thou hast a few names even in Sardis which have not defiled their garments; and they shall walk with me in white: for they are worthy.

¶ He that overcometh, the same shall be clothed in white raiment; and I will not blot out his name out of the book of life, but I will confess his name before my Father, and before his angels.

¶ He that hath an ear, let him hear what the Spirit saith unto the churches. Ch. 3:1-6

ARDIS, OF ALL THE CITIES USED IN JOHN'S ALLEGORY OF SPIRITUAL evolution, is the one most closely associated with ruling power.

The city lay north-east of Ephesus on a spur of Mount Tmolus and its history went back some one thousand years before Christ. It was taken by Alexander in 334 BC and then under the Seleucid dynasty became an administrative center, which subsequently comprised the capital of a Roman federation. The goddess adpoted by Sardis was Cybele, who was represented by two lions, giving us the astrological connection with Leo.

Sir William Ramsay, the early twentieth-century historian, tells us this about the association with lions:

"The lion, as type of the oldest Lydian coins, was certainly adopted, because it was the favorite animal and the symbol of the Sardian goddess. The Anatolian goddess, when envisaged in the form of Cybele, was regularly associated with a pair of lions or a single lion."

The characteristics of Leo are courage, dominance and self-expression, giving us our first hints as to the allegory intended. The sign that lies opposite Leo on the zodiac is Aquarius, and we can make this link with Sardis also from a reference made by Ramsay, which is connected to the inscription used on the coins in Sardis at the time – "Sardis the First Metropolis of Asia, and of Lydia and of Hellenism." Ramsay connects this in the following way:

"Hellenism in this sense was not a racial fact, but a general type of aspiration and aims, implying a certain freedom in development of the individual consciousness and in social and political organisation."

The main characteristics of Aquarius are a search for freedom within a social environment.

Here we are guided into the fifth stage of human evolution, which, if we remember, involves the "subtle plane" where the fear of death disappears and the individual experiences a closer connection with "the whole," or "oneness" with existence.

The letter to the churches of Sardis lifts, prophetically, the fate of mankind to still greater heights – to a position beyond the seven stars to the seven spirits of God.

These things saith he that hath the seven Spirits of God, and the seven stars; I know thy works, that thou hast a name that thou livest, and art dead.

It would be reasonable to assume from the above text that the seven Spirits of God which man will inherit at the fifth stage of evolution are those given to us by Paul in his Epistle to Timothy: power (or will), love and wisdom (or a sound mind), at the higher level. These were the very basis for the Trinitarian concept of Father, Son and Holy Ghost. In order to reach stage five and find wholeness we need to integrate these higher powers with the lower ones which are derived from nature – the four elements of Fire, which we can interpret as striving (or desire), Earth, which we can call crystallization, Air, which we can call friendship and social integration, and finally Water or cohesion (or attachment). Once these lower, human spirits are brought together through spiritual understanding, we reach the fifth level of spiritual evolution and become whole and connected with our world and our inner consciousness.

Opposite: The Phrygian goddess of fertility and immortality, Cybele, with her dragons. Known to the Greeks as Aphrodite, and to the Semites as Ishtar, she was an incarnation of ancient Sumer's Inanna, "Queen of Heaven and Earth." Woodcut by Jost Amman, sixteenth century, Nuremberg.

The last two letters of John – to Philadelphia and Laodicea – appear in this sequence in the Authorized Version of the Bible. The official canon of the New Testament, however, was only fixed in the fourth century AD. Earlier traditions had the books of the Bible in different orders, and there were many more books. If we read the letters of John in Revelation against the backdrop of what we know about the sources he drew upon, they make better and deeper sense in the order that follows, particularly in the light of our understanding of the Perennial Philosophy and the seven levels of human consciousness, with the letter to Laodicea preceding the letter to Philadelphia.

6. Laodicea

The letter to Laodicea brings us closer to the promised state of perfection. When we waken to the witness within, the sign of Scorpio will bring economic integration to the planet – global cash flow in the right direction. *Above and opposite:* Representations of Taurus and Scorpio, the astrological signs most closely associated with the city of Laodicea. Combined they herald the harnessing of wealth creation by wisdom.

And unto the angel of the church of the Laodiceans write; These things saith the Amen, the faithful and true witness, the beginning of the creation of God;

¶ I know thy works, that thou art neither cold nor hot: I would thou wert cold or hot.

¶ So then because thou art lukewarm, and neither cold nor hot, I will spue thee out of my mouth.

¶ Because thou sayest, I am rich, and increased with goods, and have need of nothing; and knowest not that thou art wretched, and miserable, and poor, and blind, and naked:

¶ I counsel thee to buy of me gold tried in the fire, that thou mayest be rich; and white raiment, that thou mayest be clothed, and that the shame of thy nakedness do not appear; and anoint thine eyes with eyesalve, that thou mayest see.

¶ As many as I love, I rebuke and chasten: be zealous therefore, and repent.

¶ Behold, I stand at the door, and knock: if any man hear my voice, and open the door, I will come in to him, and will sup with him, and he with me.

¶ To him that overcometh will I grant to sit with me in my throne, even as I also overcame, and am set down with my Father in his throne.

¶ He that hath an ear, let him hear what the Spirit saith unto the churches. Ch. 3:14-22

TO MOST OF US THIS PART OF REVELATION IS AN EXAMPLE OF WHY people generally would never hope to make sense of the Bible. It is obscure and apparently almost gibberish, but perhaps a little explanation of a few of the terms may bring these passages towards better comprehension. We can begin with the following line:

These things saith the Amen, the faithful and true witness, the beginning of the creation of God…

The Hebrew word "Amen" means "so be it" – the last word. The last word in our spiritual evolution is: "The faithful and true witness."

The term "witness" is used extensively in Eastern traditions of spiritual understanding, and implies the ultimate "watcher," or that which observes all. We could, for the purposes of simplicity, call the witness instead, the soul – that which is always aware, the "watcher" in each of us.

John brings this into the letter to Laodicea as the introductory point – when

we are totally at one with the Witness in us, enlightenment is close by.

In order to go further into the verses we need first to take a look at the astrological connections that Laodicea might assume.

Laodicea was founded by Antiochus II, grandson of Seleucus I, founder of the Seleucid dynasty. Antiochus named the city after his wife Laodice.

We can find the astrological associations of the city from its well-known commercial practices, for the city quickly gained a great reputation for commerce, and in fact became the banking and financial exchange center for the Roman Emperors. The sign of Taurus best represents these characteristics – the psychological impulse to accumulate. Taurus is seen as the sign which rules virility and increase. Its opposite on the zodiac is Scorpio, which in turn balances the city's characteristics with resourcefulness and rejuvenation – the seed to bring still more wealth and success.

The deity most closely associated with the city is Zeus, the supreme god of the Greeks, protector of laws and morality. This wise sovereign gives us a symbol of leadership.

Power and money are seen for what they really are – not something to be accumulated as ends in themselves but merely the outer representations of inner creativity. Money is the material expression of psychological energy. We have the energy and the life and therefore we can simply use money as a device to help us create.

We could say that this Taurus/Scorpio indication is the balance between the creativity of humanity and the tension which makes it happen. The sign of Scorpio also indicates sexuality, and sexuality contains always a tension related to creating life. But this is a two-edged device. On the one side it creates a tension in us that can be expressed through the sexual act. Thereby, as far as nature is concerned, producing another child and so another opportunity for higher consciousness – the expression of God, if you like. On the other side, it manifests a higher creativity that will eventually lead to godliness, or enlightenment. The desire of life is to awaken, and in this sixth stage of evolutionary growth mankind wakes up to its inner truth – to god within.

John describes this stage as *neither hot nor cold but lukewarm* and this is a reference to the result of coming to the middle way – the balance which produces a lack of emotional swing, a lack of moods and psychological problems. In a state of *satori* (a spontaneous experience of spiritual awakening) the individual could simply sit and do nothing, but Jesus tells us that we have to

Golden opportunities –
United Nations headquarters in the
financial powerhouse of New York.

use the new-found power to continue creating new ways to live.

The letter also makes allegorical mention of the alchemist's gold, "tried in the fire," and the turning of base metal into refined and precious gold. As we have seen earlier, the alchemical art symbolized the process of becoming enlightened.

7. Philadelphia

And to the angel of the church in Philadelphia write; These things saith he that is holy, he that is true, he that hath the key of David, he that openeth, and no man shutteth; and shutteth, and no man openeth;

¶ I know thy works: behold, I have set before thee an open door, and no man can shut it; for thou hast a little strength, and hast kept my word, and hast not denied my name.

¶ Behold, I will make them of the synagogue of Satan, which say they are Jews, and are not, but do lie; behold, I will make them to come and worship before thy feet, and to know that I have loved thee.

¶ Because thou hast kept the word of my patience, I also will keep thee from the hour of temptation, which shall come upon all the world, to try them that dwell upon the earth.

¶ Behold, I come quickly: hold that fast which thou hast, that no man take thy crown.

¶ Him that overcometh will I make a pillar in the temple of my God, and he shall go no more out: and I will write upon him the name of my God, and the name of the city of my God, which is new Jerusalem, which cometh down out of heaven from my God: and I will write upon him my new name.

¶ He that hath an ear, let him hear what the Spirit saith unto the churches. Ch. 3:7-13

THE FINAL LETTER TO THE CHURCH OF PHILADELPHIA TAKES US TO THE ultimate evolutionary stage – full knowledge of consciousness, a state beyond duality. In order to understand this better we can take a closer look at the city of Philadelphia and its history and associations.

From the very beginning Philadelphia was seen as a monument to the possibility of divinity within mankind. The Greek word "philadephus" means "one who loves his brother" and the city was founded to commemorate the devotion of Attalus II for his brother Eumenes II, whom he succeeded as King of Pergamum.

Founded in around 150 BC, it was situated on high ground and formed a perfect geographical position for trade. It was known as the gateway to the East because of its position at a junction of routes to Mysia, Lydia and Phrygia. It also was connected by road to Rome.

We can suppose that for John, Philadelphia would have epitomized the ideal of a city which had balance, good will and good judgment. This gives us a good

Opposite: The dove, attribute of the Love Goddess and the Holy Spirit, symbolizes ultimate stage of evolutionary development for mankind – full knowledge of consciousness, a state beyond duality.

allegory for the final stage of human spiritual evolution – that of enlightenment, the ultimate consciousness, a state that brings perfect balance. At this stage, according to all Eastern and Western religious traditions, there is no duality, but a oneness with life and all existence. The other six letters of Revelation can be exemplified by the opposites of the zodiac signs – Leo and Aquarius, or Gemini and Sagittarius, for example. Here, in each case, we have characteristics that are essentially in opposition to one another, whereas in the final stage of human evolution we become one with existence – enlightened.

Put simply we become holy, the word holy deriving from the Old English *hál*, "whole" or integrated and complete. This is also the root of the words "hale" and "heal."

The letter goes on to praise the attainment of the ultimate truth. One important line leads us to a recurring theme of Judeo-Christian belief – that of the so-called "[Second] Coming."

... behold, I have set before thee an open door, and no man can shut it...

This open door, which is spoken of in other parts of the Bible, specifically by John in his Gospel, is the door through which Christ-consciousness, or divinity, or satori, or awareness, or enlightenment – call it what you will – can come.

The concept, upon which so much belief rests today, of an actual physical arrival of Jesus Christ on earth for a second time, was, it is suggested, never the true intention of Jesus' teaching. The Second Coming would not be an earth-bound physical, "local" event, but rather a universal, un-material form. If we accept that these lines in Revelation describe the heightening of humanity to perfect conscious awareness, then the Second Coming as a physical event is an absurdity. On the other hand, if we expect goodness and perfection to exist only in heaven, concentrating all our efforts on this eventual outcome, then we ignore the possibility of realizing heaven on earth, living in the here and now.

Many words in the Bible have led humanity to make belief-structures. Take the words that indicate that when Christ appears, "all eyes shall see him." This conjures up a dramatic last-judgment scenario of Jesus standing in a halo of light on the top of a mountain with all mankind ranged out below in the valley. But the true meaning of such words could be that each of us individually will receive the Christ-consciousness within us. In other words, awakening and total awareness could be ours – here on this earthly heaven.

Jiddu Krishnamurti – whom the
Theosophists believed was the
Maitreya, or the Buddha come again
to save the world – was one example
among many men and women,
including Jesus, who reached the
final stage of enlightenment.

ost all the masters and gurus
taught similar values of
vidual Christ-consciousness.
se who found their way to
delphia. *Top left to bottom right:*
akrishna, Osho, H.W.L.Poonja,
r Baba, Ramana Maharshi, the
er. *Below:* The Russian
er G.I.Gurdjieff.

The Second Coming will occur, according to the words of Jesus himself in John's Revelation, when we all "wake up."

...and I will write upon him my new name.

This last line gives us the ultimate message of the whole book – when we reach a state of enlightenment and awakening, having lost the false persona of the ego, we will attain the same holy state as Jesus.

To give a last, slightly lighter sense to the processes suggested and outlined in this chapter, we finish with some words from G.I. Gurdjieff, the early twentieth-century Russian mystic, words that simplify the complexity of the concept outlined.

G – *Eventually, no matter what one starts with, one must go to Philadelphia. After Philadelphia all roads are the same.*

Q – *Does that mean something?*

G – *Why you ask?*

Q – *It makes me snicker, I think it cute. I wonder how much I see cuteness when you really are trying to say something.*

G – *Everyone must go to Philadelphia. Everyone thinks I mean American Philadelphia. But...To understand this, they must discover true meaning of "Philadelphia." Everyone must go to "City of Brotherly love," then all roads are the same.*

Gurdjieff was known as "G" to the writer and disciple P.D.Ouspensky.

(Secret Talks with Mr. G)

And so now we can begin to look at the apocalypse itself – the revelation of human life on earth.

The Architecture of the New World – Symbols of Perfection

IVEN THE STRUCTURE OF THE SEVEN LETTERS TO THE CHURCHES IN ASIA, an understanding of the astrological references, and some knowledge of the symbols in the original text, we can begin to look at the picture drawn by Revelation, and to find the overall story that relates to our past, our present, and our future. It begins to emerge that Revelation can be interpreted as a complete pathway for humanity to follow – a kind of evolutionary track upon which we must inevitably step. This track moves from a beginning made up of hopes, dreams and aspirations, through suffering and collapse, or Armageddon, and then eventual realization and nirvana. Apocalypse, means literally "revelation" – the revealing of the truth; not, as is popularly believed, disaster.

We start our colorful and dramatic journey through the remaining chapters of Revelation with the beginning of a plan for the world which was seen by Jesus and written by John as the ideal and inevitable place in which mankind could fulfill its promise. The picture is painted with a broad brush in this chapter, and then filled in at the end of the book. In order to set our own scene for the future, we need first to sketch out this fabulous picture of perfection, for in subtle ways, as we will see, it actually does create a real potential scenario, though perhaps in somewhat exaggerated terms, setting a seemingly impossible target. For the moment we can suspend our disbelief and sample the poetic symbolism of these early lines, for it gives us a feeling for why the language was so ornate. Later in the book we will give a clearer and more modern shape when we draw up the plan for the new world, when the description is amplified in a later chapter of Revelation.

We are, in the twentieth century, more accustomed to the symbolism of images such as that of this World War II poster – showing a bombing raid over Germany – than the one that appears overleaf.

A moment of peace following turbulence in the heavens.

… Come up hither, and I will shew thee things which must be hereafter.

¶ And immediately I was in the spirit: and, behold, a throne was set in heaven, and one sat on the throne.

¶ And he that sat was to look upon like a jasper and a sardine stone: and there was a rainbow round about the throne, in sight like unto an emerald.

¶ And round about the throne were four and twenty seats: and upon the seats I saw four and twenty elders sitting, clothed in white raiment; and they had on their heads crowns of gold.

¶ And out of the throne proceeded lightnings and thunderings and voices: and there were seven lamps of fire burning before the throne, which are the seven Spirits of God.

¶ And before the throne there was a sea of glass like unto crystal: and in the midst of the throne, and round about the throne, were four beasts full of eyes before and behind.

¶ And the first beast was like a lion, and the second beast like a calf, and the third beast had a face as a man, and the fourth beast was like a flying eagle. Ch. 4:1-7

The scene that is set for us can be interpreted as a magnificent inspired, astrological blueprint – a dramatic theater of the heavens and earth.

We are told of a throne with a mighty presence sat upon it, overseeing everything lying before it. And this powerful entity is said to be like a "jasper" and a "sardine stone." Within Babylonian, Greek and Roman cultures, the jasper (or sardine) stone symbolized birth and fertility because of its quality of appearing to reproduce itself when broken. The fractured jasper stone seems to create new light and new precious stones out of the fracturing, and the Greeks, Babylonians and Romans used its symbolism to describe holy rebirth. In this first description by John of the new world, the jasper is representative of the power of God to give birth. As we will learn later in the text of Revelation (chapter twenty-one), the jasper stone forms one of twelve precious and semi-precious stones which set the foundations of the new world, each one offering a symbolic connotation, and each one connected to one of the planets of the zodiac. But for the moment we are given only the very beginning of the "ground plan."

The rainbow about the throne can be interpreted as symbolizing light and the connection between heaven and earth. John was part of the alternative, rabbinical interpretive Judaism which would give rise to the Talmud, according to which the rainbow was created on the sixth day to signify that connection. To the Greeks, the rainbow was the sign of the goddess Iris, who acted as messenger to the gods, and so it was associated with the reconciliation of the gods and humanity. In the Middle Ages the Iris flower and therefore the rainbow were symbols of the Virgin Mary.

Above: The water and tree of life, Lincoln College Manuscript.
Opposite: William Blake's depiction of the twenty-four elders casting their crowns before the Divine Throne, *c.* 1803-5.

And finally, in this powerful single verse of Revelation we are told that God on the throne was *in sight like unto an emerald.* The emerald is rich in symbolism – according to sources such as the *Herder Dictionary of Symbols* – implying fertility, moistness, the moon and spring. The Romans attributed it to the goddess Venus, and in later medieval beliefs it became synonymous with hell and the powers of evil. For the Christians in its purer form, once exorcised of its evil power, it signified perfection, belief and immortality.

So here we begin our extraordinary picture of the new world order, the hoped-for ideal, with a description of the seat of the perfect world – fertility, purity, immortality, love and power.

And next we find more symbols of ancient power:

And round about the throne were four and twenty seats: and upon the seats I saw four and twenty elders sitting, clothed in white raiment; and they had on their heads crowns of gold.

Four and twenty seats are arrayed about the city, with four and twenty elders upon them. The number twenty-four could signify the hours in the day and night, and the double of the perfect number twelve, could refer, among other things, to the number of the twelve apostles. And it is here that we first learn of something we will find again and again in the prophecies of Revelation, the presence of a new form of government that will prevail in the new world – an oligarchic meritocracy – rule by the wise in groups, not by the "foolish" alone. Twenty-four wise elders. It is noticeably not mentioned whether they are men or women – simply that they are old and wise. They are given white clothing for purity and are crowned with gold, the most noble of metals – ductile, shining, capable of polish (always improvable), proof against heat and acid – a symbol of immutability, eternity and perfectibility. Being the color of the sun it is also a symbol of insight and knowledge, and for the Christians it meant especially love. In the alchemical beliefs of medieval Europe, the quest of all those who attempted to discover the way to transform base metal into gold, was a quest for purity and enlightenment – purification of the soul.

Such rich symbolism is intrinsic to these deceptively simple lines, forming the basis of the new world which John predicted would come. And so the story continues to unfold.

And out of the throne proceeded lightnings and thunderings and voices: and there were seven lamps of fire burning before the throne, which are the seven Spirits of God.

This mighty throne sent forth the elements of the earth and sky – lightning and thunder. Both were symbols of divine power, of God's wrathful judgment –

the power of punishment and the giving of light. This symbolism had been taken also from the Greeks and Romans, and Oriental cultures such as the Persians, who saw these mighty forms of nature as symbols also of fertility, with lightning having a phallic significance. Thus great power is held in the hands of the throne, given to the twenty-four elders of the new world.

And then we learn of the magic number seven, for there are *seven lamps of fire burning before the throne, which are the seven Spirits of God.*

The number seven has been regarded since antiquity as a holy number, probably originally because of the four phases of the moon, each of which continues for seven days, thereby giving the number an aura of completion. In Buddhism there are seen to be seven different heavens, and the Chinese regard the seven stars of the Great Bear as being connected with the seven bodily openings and the seven openings of the human heart.

In the very earliest Babylonian observations of the skies there were seen to be seven planets, including the Sun and the Moon, and these were believed to be the divine expressions of cosmic order. In Mesopotamian mythology there were seven evil demons. In Greece the number seven was sacred to Apollo, there were the seven Hesperides, the seven gates of Thebes, the seven sons of Helios, the seven sons and seven daughters of Niobe, the seven wise men, and the "Seven against Thebes." We still speak of the seven wonders of the world. In Judaism in particular the number seven held the greatest divinity.

Throughout the Bible we find the number repeated in all manner of contexts – seven tribes, seven seals, seven heavens, seven days of creation. Even the division of seven – three and a half – is regarded as having significance, this time for evil – a sign of Satan's broken power. In medieval folklore the number seven turns up again and again to signify either good or bad fortune.

In these lines of Revelation, God is given seven Spirits which relate to the seven candles on the altar of every early Roman church of the time.

And before the throne there was a sea of glass like unto crystal: and in the midst of the throne, and round about the throne, were four beasts full of eyes before and behind.

The sea of glass like unto crystal could symbolize the presence of divine transparency. Glass was seen as being representative of purity because it had the ability to let through light – especially in crystal form, for crystal fractured light and sent it in all directions – without being affected. Because crystal does not burn, but can ignite a flame when sunlight passes through it, in Christianity it symbolizes the Immaculate Conception.

And the first beast was like a lion, and the second beast like a calf, and the third beast had a face as a man, and the fourth beast was like a flying eagle.

As we have seen, these four animals most likely represent the four main signs of the zodiac – the lion is Leo, the calf is Taurus, the "face as a man" is Aquarius, the water-bearer, and the eagle is Scorpio. The four "stones" of the "foundation" of the astrological heavens provide a basis for the new world, always connected to everything in existence, no longer isolated by fear and anxiety.

With this first description of the new world we can imagine for our future, John goes on to provide the most important aspect of the character of the world – the vital feature of its fundamental personality.

From the Lincoln College Manuscript:
Top: The book with seven seals.
Above: The lamb opening the book.
Opposite, above: The opening of the sixth seal. *Opposite, below:* The new song, the four beasts and elders adore God.

And I saw in the right hand of him that sat on the throne a book written within and on the backside, sealed with seven seals.

¶ And I saw a strong angel proclaiming with a loud voice, Who is worthy to open the book, and to loose the seals thereof?

¶ And no man in heaven, nor in earth, neither under the earth, was able to open the book, neither to look thereon....

¶ And one of the elders saith unto me, Weep not: behold, the Lion of the tribe of Juda, the Root of David, hath prevailed to open the book, and to loose the seven seals thereof.

¶ And I beheld, and, lo, in the midst of the throne and of the four beasts, and in the midst of the elders, stood a Lamb as it had been slain, having seven horns and seven eyes, which are the seven Spirits of God sent forth into all the earth.

¶ And he came and took the book out of the right hand of him that sat upon the throne.

¶ And when he had taken the book, the four beasts and four and twenty elders fell down before the Lamb, having every one of them harps, and golden vials full of odours, which are the prayers of saints.

¶ And they sung a new song, saying, Thou art worthy to take the book, and to open the seals thereof: for thou wast slain, and hast redeemed us to God by thy blood out of every kindred, and tongue, and people, and nation;

¶ And hast made us unto our God kings and priests: and we shall reign on the earth.

¶ And I beheld, and I heard the voice of many angels round about the throne and the beasts and the elders: and the number of them was ten thousand times ten thousand, and thousands of thousands;

¶ Saying with a loud voice, Worthy is the Lamb that was slain to receive power, and riches, and wisdom, and strength, and honour, and glory, and blessing.

¶ And every creature which is in heaven, and on the earth, and under the earth, and such as are in the sea, and all that are in them, heard I saying, Blessing, and honour, and glory, and power, be unto him that sitteth upon the throne, and unto the Lamb for ever and ever.

¶ And the four beasts said, Amen. And the four and twenty elders fell down and worshipped him that liveth for ever and ever. Ch. 5:1-14

These lines can be interpreted as conveying one simple idea – that it is ultimately not a matter of physical strength or intellectual capacity, but spiritual simplicity that is needed to acquire knowledge. The wise worship the simple. The presence of a book that is hard to open is symbolic of the discovery of true knowledge being difficult to acquire. This is not the mundane knowledge we all learn in school, but a knowledge of spiritual truth.

So our city of perfection also encompasses the biblical qualities of the Lamb – meekness and submission. In Christian terms the meek literally inherit the earth. But, looking at the same words in greater depth, we can find a metaphor for the relinquishing of personal attachments on the journey towards absolute truth.

And here, Revelation's rendering of the future world ends for the moment.

The Four Horsemen

WITH CHAPTER SIX OF THE BOOK OF REVELATION, WE BEGIN THE countdown to the apocalypse – the beginning of the actual revelation itself. And we should remember that this book of prophecy was made some two thousand years ago. We can interpret its fulfilment as being now. It could be said that we are at the center of the apocalypse. During the twentieth century we have seen already two major world wars. In World War I, more human lives were taken than ever in the history of mankind. It was seen at the time as Armageddon. In World War II, Nazi Germany became a charnel house, introducing mankind to the rationalized obscenity of the Holocaust. Now we face the threat of a nuclear apocalypse from the proliferation of nuclear weapons amongst emerging powers. In Western mythology we have had the Flood, and are promised the Fire next time.

On the following pages are visual representations of the Four Horsemen – war, pestilence, famine (poverty) and death – in each case with statistics covering the recent past and projected through to the near future. But first let us read the text of the Four Horsemen within Revelation.

Of all the symbols in the Book of Revelation, the Four Horsemen of the Apocalypse have enjoyed the greatest notoriety. *Above:* An eleventh-century Apocalypse showing the Four Horsemen. *Opposite:* Albrecht Dürer's dramatic woodcut, in the series of the **Apocalypse** (1498), shows them in an oblique gallop.

And I saw when the Lamb opened one of the seals, and I heard, as it were the noise of thunder, one of the four beasts saying, Come and see.

¶ And I saw, and behold a white horse: and he that sat on him had a bow; and a crown was given unto him: and he went forth conquering, and to conquer.

¶ And when he had opened the second seal, I heard the second beast say, Come and see.

¶ And there went out another horse that was red: and power was given to him that sat thereon to take peace from the earth, and that they should kill one another: and there was given unto him a great sword.

¶ And when he had opened the third seal, I heard the third beast say, Come and see. And I beheld, and lo a black horse; and he that sat on him had a pair of balances in his hand.

¶ And I heard a voice in the midst of the four beasts say, A measure of wheat for a penny, and three measures of barley for a penny; and see thou hurt not the oil and the wine.

¶ And when he had opened the fourth seal, I heard the voice of the fourth beast say, Come and see.

The work-horses of modern warfare.
Helicopters riding into battle over Kuwait.

¶ And I looked, and behold a pale horse: and his name that sat on him was Death, and Hell followed with him. And power was given unto them over the fourth part of the earth, to kill with sword, and with hunger, and with death, and with the beasts of the earth.

¶ And when he had opened the fifth seal, I saw under the altar the souls of them that were slain for the word of God, and for the testimony which they held:

¶ And they cried with a loud voice, saying, How long, O Lord, holy and true, dost thou not judge and avenge our blood on them that dwell on the earth?

¶ And white robes were given unto every one of them; and it was said unto them, that they should rest yet for a little season, until their fellowservants also and their brethren, that should be killed as they were, should be fulfilled. Ch. 6:1-11

These lines are amongst the most famous of all those in Revelation, for they describe the four horsemen of the apocalypse – the four horsemen that bring the greatest fears of humanity to fruition – war (white), pestilence (red), famine (black) and death (pale).

These four horsemen have captured our imagination because they represent fears that have been projected onto the apocalypse. But perhaps the real intention of the writer of the lines of Revelation was not only death in the way that we are normally accustomed to understanding it. We have seen that the literal meaning of "apocalypse" is not physical death. It is revelation of the truth. The four horsemen of the apocalypse are not just "killers" in a literal sense – the "killing" that they do could also be symbolic. During almost the whole of the twentieth century humanity has been in the eye of the physical manifestation of the apocalyptic storm. Perhaps we are about to emerge into the "broad sunlit uplands."

On following pages we have drawn maps tracing the progressions of the four methods of killing which humanity has experienced and which it will continue to experience through to the next century. These maps plot the changes in war, famine (poverty), population growth, and disease through to the twenty-first century.

We will take each of these four horsemen in turn and look at the implications, both from an allegorical and a literal point of view. The maps provide statistics and details for each of the four categories, and, using past and present figures, project the trends in each case through to the twenty-first century. We begin with war, in which we trace the process of human conflict and its evolution from past through present into future.

The External Reality

The White Horseman

BETWEEN TWO THOUSAND YEARS AGO and the beginning of the twentieth century, wars were essentially local affairs. They were battles rather than wars, and tended to impact on only relatively small segments of national populations. Even the major conflicts between rival imperial powers such as Britain, France or Spain, were made up of campaigns fought on land between professional armies or at sea amongst a relatively small number of ships which bombarded one another in a duel of might that decided the fate of a whole country.

World War I was unprecedented in its scale. It influenced enormous segments of the global population and had devastating economic consequences, to say nothing of the shocking effect on the human psyche. The first of the maps on these pages shows the battle lines of the Western Front. The most astonishing aspect of this war was the dreadful slaughter for no apparent reason or effect. The journalists of the time all used the word Armageddon to describe the situation. The so-called "front" line remained virtually unchanged during the greater part of the conflict – almost three years – when none of the offensives by either side served to gain more than a few thousand yards, despite a colossal expenditure of ammunition, blood and human life.

World War I was the very first conflict of any size in which the number of killed in battle exceeded the number dying of disease. Until then, wars tended to give rise to outbreaks of epidemic illnesses such as typhus or dysentery because of the concentration of men in one place for a campaign. People within the battle areas died at more or less the same rate, whether they were involved in

War – the First Horseman of the Apocalypse.
From the Lincoln College Manuscript.
Unexpectedly, war will diminish during the
latter years of the twentieth century.

During World War I, some four million men were slaughtered over three years for the sake of a few hundred yards of territory – probably the greatest waste of life ever.

combat or not. The predisposition to sickness was exacerbated by the frequent failures to ensure adequate supplies. Now that millions of soldiers were assembled successfully and, thanks to the railways, the problems of supply were solved, men died on the field of battle on a scale never before seen. The invention of the machine gun added further confusion and loss of life, for the commanders were unable to fathom any way of dealing with this weapon except to hurl men at it in "human waves."

The stultifying nature of the war was demoralizing and it led to the widespread and profound disillusionment which characterized the post-war period. For those middle three and a half years of the war, the static trench warfare on the Western Front was probably the best representation of hell that mankind had managed so far to invent.

And yet, within the short space of only two decades, as though humanity had learned nothing from entering the gates of hell, World War II broke out and the whole bizarre madness of humans killing one another on a massive scale began again.

But this time there was a difference, for World War II, begun by the insanity of one individual, ended with the insanity of another, when the first atomic nuclear device was dropped on the enemy. The maps showing the effects of

TRENCH WARFARE: THE WESTERN FRONT IN THE FIRST WORLD WAR
October 1914 to February 1918

The frontline remained essentially unchanged throughout this period, the only shift of any consequence being the Germans' planned withdrawal to the Hindenburg line in February – March 1917. United States forces started joining the Allies towards the end of 1917, completing their build-up in Spring 1918 in time for the offensive that broke the stalemate.

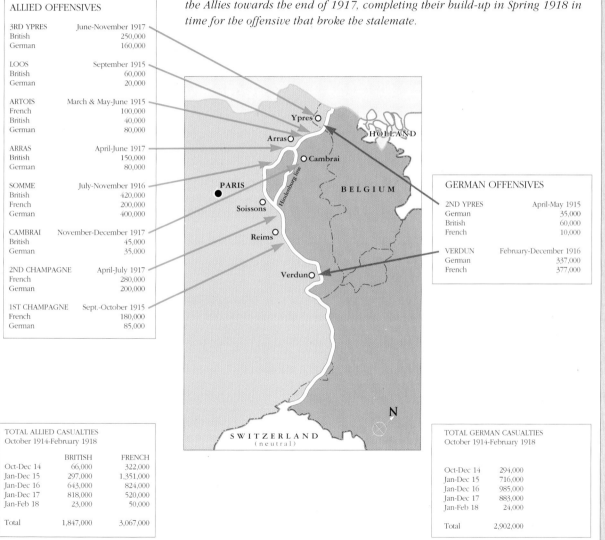

ALLIED OFFENSIVES

3RD YPRES	June-November 1917
British	250,000
German	160,000

LOOS	September 1915
British	60,000
German	20,000

ARTOIS	March & May-June 1915
French	100,000
British	40,000
German	80,000

ARRAS	April-June 1917
British	150,000
German	80,000

SOMME	July-November 1916
British	420,000
French	200,000
German	400,000

CAMBRAI	November-December 1917
British	45,000
German	35,000

2ND CHAMPAGNE	April-July 1917
French	280,000
German	200,000

1ST CHAMPAGNE	Sept.-October 1915
French	180,000
German	85,000

GERMAN OFFENSIVES

2ND YPRES	April-May 1915
German	35,000
British	60,000
French	10,000

VERDUN	February-December 1916
German	337,000
French	377,000

Map labels: Ypres, Arras, HOLLAND, Cambrai, PARIS, Hindenburg line, BELGIUM, Soissons, Reims, Verdun, SWITZERLAND (neutral), N

TOTAL ALLIED CASUALTIES
October 1914-February 1918

	BRITISH	FRENCH
Oct-Dec 14	66,000	322,000
Jan-Dec 15	297,000	1,351,000
Jan-Dec 16	643,000	824,000
Jan-Dec 17	818,000	520,000
Jan-Feb 18	23,000	50,000
Total	1,847,000	3,067,000

TOTAL GERMAN CASUALTIES
October 1914-February 1918

Oct-Dec 14	294,000
Jan-Dec 15	716,000
Jan-Dec 16	985,000
Jan-Dec 17	883,000
Jan-Feb 18	24,000
Total	2,902,000

nuclear bombing on the following pages illustrate a benchmark in human destructiveness. They are based on the effect of the first nuclear strike on the island city of Hiroshima. From the standpoint of the external reality of the apocalypse predicted by Jesus, the appearance of the nuclear bomb was a highly significant development.

The Hiroshima mission, planned to bring the Japanese "to heel," was flawlessly executed. The bomb was dropped exactly at the intended aiming point, and because Hiroshima is built on a flat river delta, the relatively small bomb – known as "Little Boy" – with an explosive force of only twelve kilotons, did maximum damage. The next mission, a few days later, was fraught right from the start. There were technical problems on the aircraft. There was a failure of the accompanying aircraft to come to the rendezvous, which caused delay. There was smoke from a previous, conventional, bombing raid over the primary target, Kokura, so they had to swing to the secondary target, Nagasaki, and that was obscured by cloud. The bombardier was forced to use the only aiming point that he could visualize, the Urakami Stadium, and that was more than two kilometers north of the favored aiming point at the head of the bay. The result of this was that the "Fat Man" bomb, though nearly twice as powerful as "Little Boy," caused only a comparable amount of damage and the eastern

The use of atomic bombs at the end of World War II represented the peak of warfare during the twentieth century. The maps on this page show the areas in each case that were completely destroyed by the two single 12-kiloton bombs.

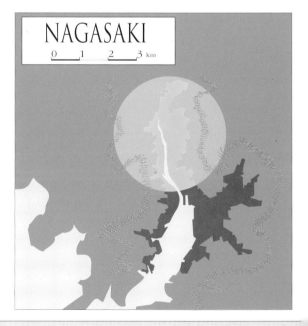

THE ATOMIC STRIKES AGAINST JAPAN – AUGUST 1945

MISSION	HIROSHIMA	NAGASAKI
Date	August 6	August 9
Aircraft	B-29 Enola Gay	B-29 Bock's Car
Take-off time (Tinian)	0245	0256
Targets		
Primary	Hiroshima	Kokura*
Secondary	Kokura*	Nagasaki
Bombing Alt.	31,000ft.	31,000ft.
AP	Aioi Bridge	Urakami Stadiam
WEAPON		
Code Name	Little Boy	Fat Man
Weight	4 tons	4.5 tons
Length	3 meters	3.5 meters
Diameter	0.7 meters	1.5 meters
Fissile material	42kg. Uranium 235	5kg. Plutonium 239
TNT equivalent	12,500 tons	22,000 tons
Detonation	8.15 am **	11.02**
Altitude	580 meters	503 meters
Ground zero	550 meters. SE of AP	210 metersNE of AP
HUMAN TOLL		
City Population	325,000	200,000
Died immediately	60,000	30,000
Died to end '45	100,000	50,000

* Now part of Kitakyushu, a conurbation formed by the merger of 5 adjacent cites in 1963.

** Local time: Tinian times 9.15 and 12.02.

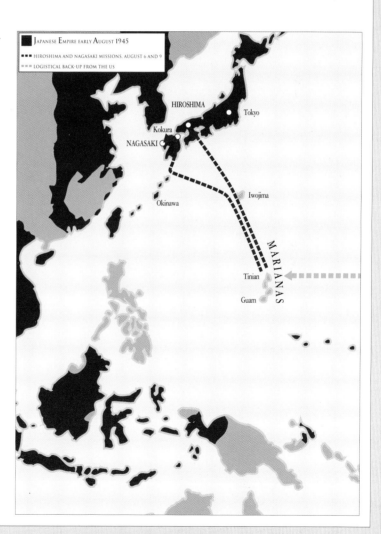

JAPANESE EMPIRE EARLY AUGUST 1945

■■■ HIROSHIMA AND NAGASAKI MISSIONS, AUGUST 6 AND 9

■■■ LOGISTICAL BACK-UP FROM THE US

HIROSHIMA
Tokyo
Kokura
NAGASAKI
Okinawa
Iwojima
MARIANAS
Tinian
Guam

part of Nagasaki, which was protected from the blast by the hills between the two halves of the town, was relatively unscathed.

Japan showed no sign of surrendering after the dropping of the first bomb. After the second bomb, we are told by historians, stubbornness nearly prevailed. Had Japan not surrendered, there were more versions of "Fat Man" coming off the production line at the rate of one bomb a week through the remainder of 1945.

The four maps, one each of the centers of London, New York, Munich and Moscow, illustrate the destructive potential of modern nuclear devices used in anger. Each map has a number of concentric circles indicating the destructive radius of a one megaton warhead. To put this into perspective, the innermost circle shows the area equivalent to the zone of severe damage at Hiroshima – this would be totally flattened with nothing alive or standing. The middle and outer circles show the graduated effects of a modern one megaton bomb – fifty times the size of the bombs dropped on Japan. The radius of destruction is not actually so much greater than the smaller bombs – about 5 miles as opposed to 1.5 miles. The extra power within a larger nuclear bomb (that is, the difference between the equivalent of twelve thousand tons of TNT and one million tons of TNT) inflates a sphere rather than a circle – in other words it bursts upwards and sideways more than it does downwards and sideways, and so "wastes" much of its force.

Top: Hiroshima, aftermath. The devastation was far beyond anything even imagined by mankind.
Above: Nuclear weapon of the "Little Boy" type detonated over Hiroshima.

CIRCLES OF DESTRUCTION:
Effects of a megaton airblast at 8,000 feet (2,400 meters) over:
A) London, B) New York, C) Moscow, D) Munich.

Inner (red) circle (radius 3.75km): *zone of complete destruction and 90% mortality.*
Outer (red) circle (radius 7km): *zone of severe damage and 50% mortality.*
Innermost (dashed) circle, (radius 2km): *zone of severe damage at Hiroshima.*

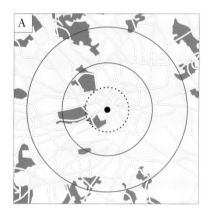

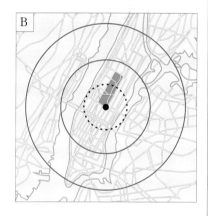

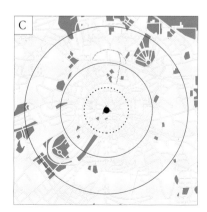

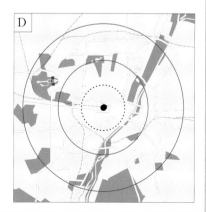

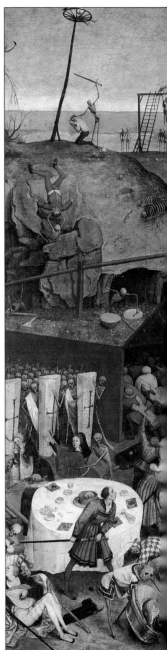

Dropped on any of these familiar cities, a one megaton bomb would probably kill up to a million people, depending on the time of day or night and the fluctuation of populations in the city centers. In addition there would be up to a million and a half injured around the edges of the circle. To completely destroy a megacity city like London, New York or Moscow would take several megaton weapons – three or four would do it.

The use of very big warheads, in the twenty-five to fifty megaton range, would not achieve the same result as several smaller ones. The larger bombs yield diminishing returns. This is partly, as we have seen, because of the geometry of spheres as against circles, and partly because, with the larger weapons, the top of the sphere goes through the top of the earth's atmosphere and a lot of the force of the explosion is vented into outer space.

Put simply, up until the present, the nuclear threat has worked. In the history of warfare, we reached a peak of slaughter during the first half of the twentieth century; then, suddenly, the incidence of death by war took a dive and has continued to drop. As mankind has developed a greater capacity for self-destruction, so it has reduced its willingness to use it.

On the basis of the evidence, the global scourge of death by war has peaked. It could be said, and hoped, that the worst is over.

Below: Pestilence – the Second Horseman. From the Lincoln College Manuscript.

Previous page, left: Atomic bomb test explosion. *Right:* Pieter Brueghel's **Triumph of Death**, from the Prado, Madrid.

The Red Horseman

PLAGUES HAVE BROUGHT SUFFERING AND TERROR TO MANKIND throughout history. Probably the most dramatic, until recently, was the bubonic or pneumonic plague, which on several occasions swept across continents claiming millions of lives.

Bubonic plague is transmitted by rat fleas, which have been infected with the bacterium *Pasteurella pestis,* from the rat population to humans. It is not by and large transmitted from humans to one another. Epidemics occur when humans and rats are in close proximity. The fleas are attracted to the heat of the human body, particularly at night during sleep. Experience in India, around the turn of the century, suggests that those who left the infected villages and slept in the fields were not infected. Those who remained in the villages and were warm in bed, were more discernible targets for the fleas.

Plague was first transmitted by the fleas to the rats, who would then develop septicemia and could thereby give a charge of infected blood back to the fleas when bitten again. When a human is bitten by an infected flea, the infection enters the lymphatic system, not

the bloodstream, and so does not give back an infective charge to the flea via septicemia. Therefore, as the rats die of the disease, the fleas die off too because there is no inter-infection going on. And as humans do not generally infect one another, the death of the last infected rat meant the end of the plague in that place and time. Plague, therefore, tended to come in a massive dose throughout an area such as Europe, and then gradually die out and disappear for a long time.

The maps on these and the following pages show the awesome spread of the Black Death across the trade routes of Europe between 1347 and 1351, taking a greater toll of life than any other disease or war up to that time. In Britain, between one third and a half of the entire population died from this particular epidemic.

The plague was transmitted mainly by sea, or where there was a lot of shipping, as the rats on boats and in harbors carried the disease from one area to another. Once it got into the heart of a continent like Europe, it tended to die out for the reasons we have already shown.

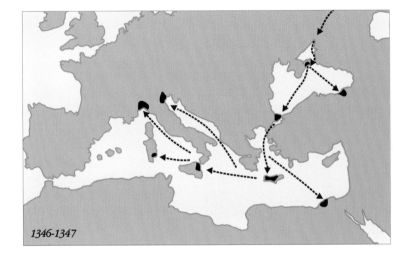

1346-1347

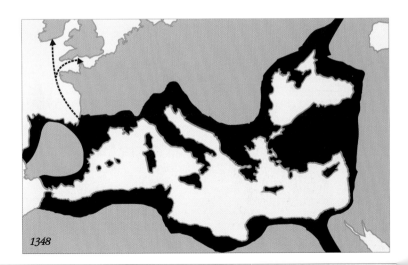

1348

The maps on these pages show the spread of the Black Death across Europe during the fourteenth century. The bubonic plague had occurred in the East and in Europe several times during the Middle Ages, but never on this scale. The medical knowledge of the time gave no opportunity to prevent this astonishing disease from wiping out around forty percent of the population of Europe, as it moved from fleas to rats to humans, killing most of its victims within two to seven days of infection.

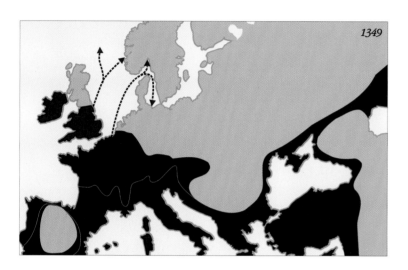

1349

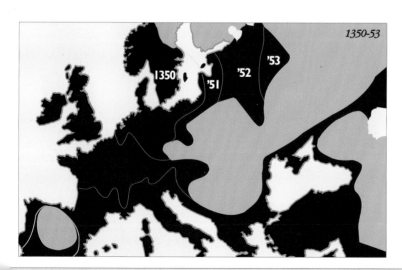

1350-53

1350 '51 '52 '53

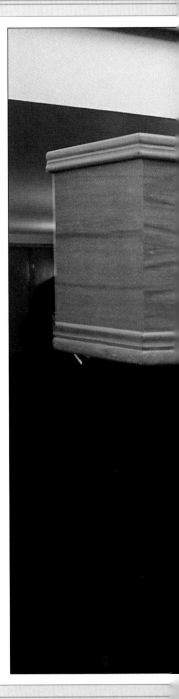

In the past the great killer was the bubonic plague. In the late twentieth century the equivalent may be AIDS. Will this be the last killer plague or will worse diseases be produced in the future?

Humanity is now experiencing the second worst plague to visit us – AIDS. What makes this disease unique and disturbing for twentieth-century medicine is the one hundred percent mortality among those it infects.

The real problem of AIDS, as opposed to the bubonic or pneumonic plagues, is that one of its modes of transmission is sexual, from human to human, striking thereby at the very "heart" of human relating. The second problem, which arises out of the first, is that we do not yet seem to be willing to discover exactly how many people are already HIV positive. Mass testing, at the time of writing, is not happening. Though, of course, each individual has the right to privacy, it would be a pity to wait until it is too late for us to keep that right.

However, although there are no official projections to this effect, it seems likely – given the tendency to ignore the situation, and the method of transmission of the disease – that much larger numbers of the human race, in all sectors of society, will be affected by the early part of the next century.

The other, most significant aspect of the work of the red horseman is that disease appears to become progressively more sophisticated. Our capacity to cure each disease that comes along is continually challenged, for each time we cure one disease, something worse appears to rear its ugly head – plague, cancer, AIDS. We may well find a cure for AIDS during the coming decades, but let us hope that there isn't a new and still more sophisticated strain of disease just around the corner.

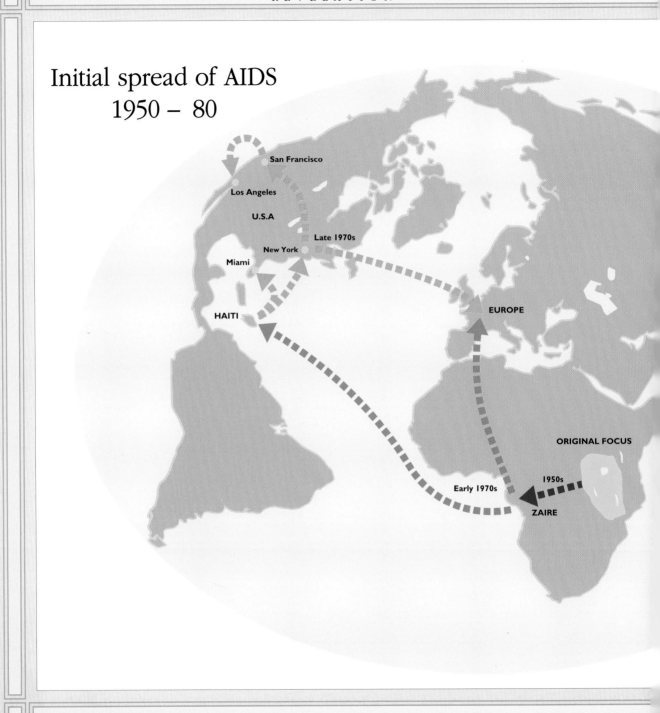

Initial spread of AIDS
1950 – 80

San Francisco

Los Angeles

U.S.A

Late 1970s

New York

Miami

HAITI

EUROPE

ORIGINAL FOCUS

1950s

Early 1970s

ZAIRE

On these pages we can see the equivalent movement of AIDS around the world. Statisticians and medical experts will tell us that AIDS comes nowhere near the disaster level of the bubonic plague, but who knows how many people are actually HIV positive today? And unlike the plague, AIDS kills *all* its victims.

Estimated number of cases worldwide
(Millions)

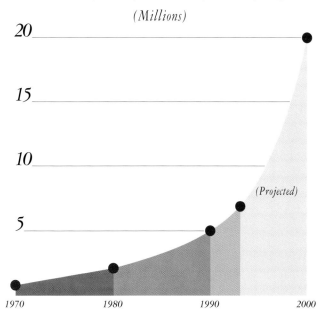

The Great Famine, Ireland

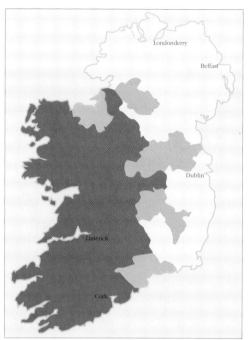

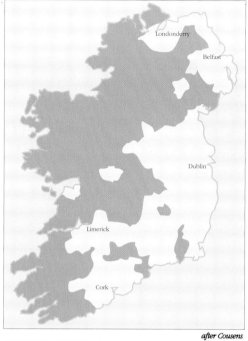

after Cousens

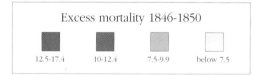

Excess mortality 1846-1850

12.5-17.4	10-12.4	7.5-9.9	below 7.5

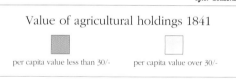

Value of agricultural holdings 1841

per capita value less than 30/-	per capita value over 30/-

Above and opposite: The correlation between poverty and famine: Ireland and Africa.

There was always food to be bought in Ireland. The problem was that the Irish rural poor had no money to buy it. Poverty, as much as natural disaster, is the harbinger of famine.

With the improvement in our ability to send aid to starving countries, there has been some small progress, thereby, in the relief of certain aspects of famine. But it is suggested that perhaps the real problem lies in the poor distribution of wealth. According to the predictions in Revelation, famine will spread into much wider areas of the world during the next century, as we shall see later in the book.

Per Capita GNP in Africa, 1991

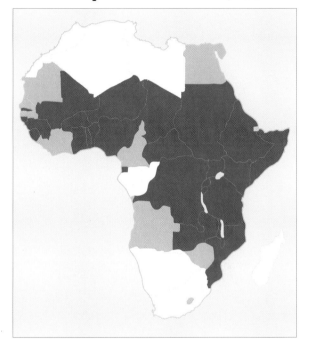

Per capita GNP

above $1,000   below $1,000   below $500

Negative Growth in Africa, 1980 – 91

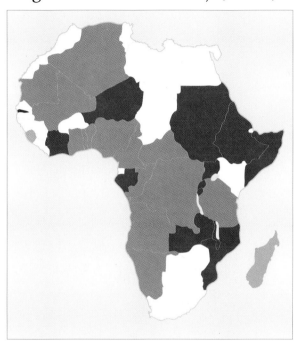

Growth per annum

-0.1 to -1.9 %   -2.0 to -4.2 %

Global change in per capita GNP 1980 – 91

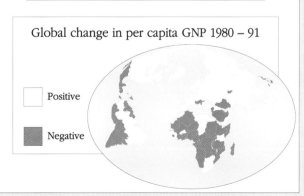

Positive

Negative

Opposite: The Irish Famine was brought about by a failure in the potato harvest throughout Britain at the time. And here again, it was not because there was no food available, but because there was no money to buy it that more than a million people died.

Above: The famines in Africa in recent years demonstrate the fatal combination of scarcity and poverty. Compared with the rest of the world, Africa has moved into negative growth and is less able to cope with emergencies like crop failure.

The Pale Horseman

FINALLY, WE COME TO THE FOURTH RIDER, ON A PALE HORSE, WHOSE name is death. We can consider this horseman as being a metaphor for the processes that determine the balance on this planet between life and death – or put another way, the balance between birth and death, namely demographics. How many living to how many dead will there be in the future? How many bodies to how many souls? Demographic trends, according to a number of sources, such as Paul Kennedy's book *Preparing for the Twenty-First Century,* indicate a massive population explosion occurring on the planet during this and the next century.

Opposite: The Fourth Horseman – Death. Lincoln College Manuscript. *Below:* William Blake's **Death on a Pale Horse,** *c.* 1800, Fitzwilliam Museum, Cambridge.

If we consider the growth of population in an historical perspective, the rate of increase is daunting. In the early nineteenth century there were some one billion of us here on earth. It had taken thousands of years to reach that level. In the next hundred years, by 1925, the population doubled to two billion. Between 1925 and 1976 – just fifty years – it doubled again to four billion. By 1990 it was at five and a half billion.

According to some demographic interpretations, the rates of growth have slowed slightly during the first few years of the 1990s, partly due to a reduction in fertility levels in many countries – men have lower levels of sperm production than they used to. Expectations at present are that eventually the population may stabilize and cease to grow at such an overwhelming rate, but this will take a very long time to happen, probably not having any impact until the middle of the twenty-first century. In the meantime, population figures will increase at breakneck speed.

Baidoa, Somalia, 1992. Removing a dead child.

Current demographic calculations set out three possible trends – low, middle and high. According to the low estimates, by the date 2025, a year when at least half of the readers of this book will still be alive, there will be seven and a half billion people on this planet. In other words, for approximately every three people around us now, there will be four.

According to the middle estimates, the figure by 2025 will be eight and a half billion people – for approximately every three people around us now, there will be four and a half. And according to the highest expectation – which is probably the most accurate, for human estimates tend to be on the low, slow level – there will be nine and a half billion people. That is, for every three people around us now, there will be almost five. The World Bank has calculated that population figures may stabilize (that is, the right number of people will be born to balance with the number of people dying) when they reach fourteen and a half billion – that is an increase of three people around us now to almost eight in the middle of the twenty-first century.

Imagine traveling to the office in the morning with two and a half times the number of cars there are today! Though, in fact, it is not so much in the West that the growth is likely to be fastest, but in Third World countries. Estimates from sources such as the British Economist indicate that Africa's population, for example, if it is not decimated by plague and famine, will be more than thr times that of Europe by 2025, whereas in 1985 it was the same.

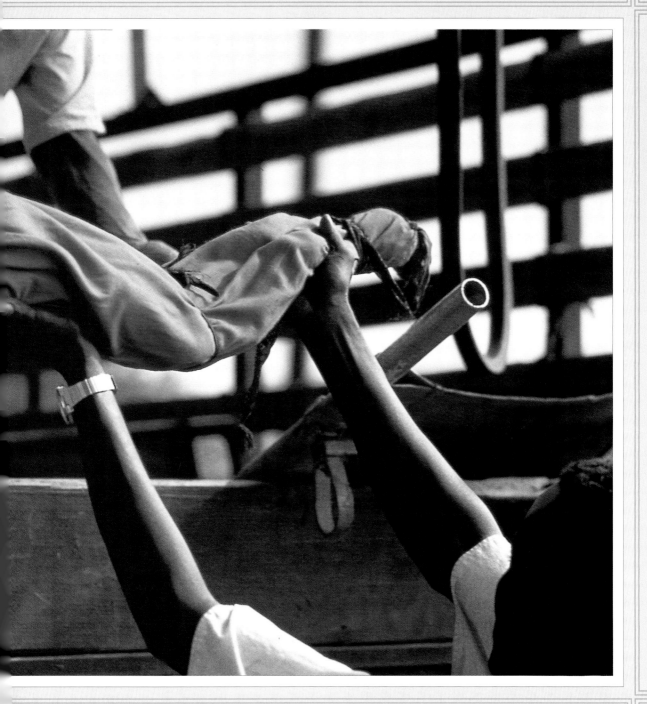

The Inner Reality

BUT ON ANOTHER LEVEL, THE HIDDEN LEVEL OF THE INTERNAL APOCALYPSE, the four horsemen can be interpreted as indicating to us also something completely different – revelation through realization.

DEATH BY WAR *And I saw, and behold a white horse: and he that sat on him had a bow; and a crown was given unto him: and he went forth conquering, and to conquer.*

Metaphorically, the power of the white horseman who carried a bow and a crown could indicate the transformation of consciousness, giving free access to higher levels of conscious freedom. White light is seen as primordial, only becoming visible when broken up into colors, and when used symbolically, as it is here, with a horse, the message can be interpreted as being about mediation or communication at a high level. The horse can be seen as the mediator between man and his message, carrying him on his quests in the world. In this way the white horse transforms our consciousness. It is significant also that the "slain" are given white robes, symbolizing their attainment of new understanding.

These white-robed people represent those who have already acquired meditation as a power for higher consciousness. We find similar references to spiritual attainment in the myths of other cultures; for example, the Native American Hopi creation story tells of a group of people who have the power to sing a certain holy song, and these people are the ones who are protected. The power to sing is again symbolic of a capacity for silence and meditation.

The astrological sign associated with the white horseman (because of the bow and crown mentioned in this verse) is Sagittarius, which symbolizes dominion and rulership, far-reaching and concerned with expanding horizons despite all obstacles.

DEATH BY PESTILENCE *And there went out another horse that was red: and power was given to him that sat thereon to take peace from the earth, and that they should kill one another: and there was given unto him a great sword.*

The color red can be interpreted most readily through its associations with blood and thereby with life-giving forces. The horse in classical mythology was seen as the mediator between man and his experience. A red horse, therefore, can be interpreted as symbolizing experience of life. The red horse-rider carries a sword with which to sever mankind from his rationalized experiences, from the rationality that is born out of that experience. This combination of man,

Left: The White Robe Brotherhood at the Osho commune in India –
thousands of individuals together sampling the inner reality.
Previous page: **The Triumph of Death,** fifteenth-century fresco,
Catalan School, National Gallery, Palermo.

mediator and sword can be seen, therefore, as representing a liberation from our analytical faculties.

The power of this horseman can be interpreted as the death of our cultivated natures – the killing of the "dis-eases" of our lower consciousness. This is not intended to be a moral judgment. This is the horseman who raises the level of the energy within the body – from base, physical energy, through to the highest form of awareness, which is enlightenment.

DEATH BY FAMINE - In a sense this horseman had the task of creating boredom! Famine, in its symbolic context could be interpreted as being a spiritual dearth created by too much rationality, or a dissatisfaction with mundane reality, with money, with society. The spiritual process, as outlined by many, including Jesus, contains frequent disillusionment. This losing of the illusions often results, in those that remain within the bounds of conventional society, in cynicism. But cynicism is not the inevitable result of a loss of illusions. If we maintain our innocence within the spiritual process, disillusionment provides joy and it is the bringing of this joy, once again through transformation, that can be seen as the task of the horseman of famine.

DEATH by whatever means, is used frequently as a symbol of the death of the ego, the end of the power of the rational capabilities to dominate the individual. We live, almost all of us, within the fixed boundaries of the society we are brought up in. We learn habits as children that are repeated over and over again – don't commit crime, don't express emotions, don't expect joy, work hard to succeed, and so on. All these constraints are seen as necessities, whereas they can also be seen as forms of unnatural conditioning. If we repeat any particular exercise often enough, it will become a habit. Shamans, for example, in Siberia, in South America, Africa and other parts of the world, learn to live consciously inside their dreams, so that the difference between waking reality and dream reality almost disappears, and they do this by habitually performing various exercises until it becomes natural.

The art of thinking and the powers of the ego are no more than habits, and when the horseman of death comes our way, he rids us of this habit so that we may find true freedom.

CHAPTER
THE
APOCALYPSE NOW—
THE PREDICTIONS

Fire and Brimstone

AS WE HAVE HINTED EARLIER, FOR EVERY INNER CHANGE, FOR EVERY SPIRITUAL apocalypse in the hearts of mankind, there is an outer apocalypse also, and chapter eight of Revelation helps us to see the beginning of the outer apocalypse, which we could be considered to be involved in during the last years of the twentieth century.

Above: The second and third trumpets sound, from the Lincoln College Manuscript.
Opposite: Aftermath of the Gulf War – minefield in Kuwait.

Previous page: UN soldiers between the Serbian and Moslem lines in Bosnia, 1994.

And the smoke of the incense, which came with the prayers of the saints, ascended up before God out of the angel's hand.

¶ And the angel took the censer, and filled it with fire of the altar, and cast it into the earth: and there were voices, and thunderings, and lightnings, and an earthquake.

¶ And the seven angels which had the seven trumpets prepared themselves to sound.

¶ The first angel sounded, and there followed hail and fire mingled with blood, and they were cast upon the earth: and the third part of trees was burnt up, and all green grass was burnt up.

¶ And the second angel sounded, and as it were a great mountain burning with fire was cast into the sea: and the third part of the sea became blood;

¶ And the third part of the creatures which were in the sea, and had life, died; and the third part of the ships were destroyed.

¶ And the third angel sounded, and there fell a great star from heaven, burning as it were a lamp, and it fell upon the third part of the rivers, and upon the fountains of waters;

¶ And the name of the star is called Wormwood: and the third part of the waters became wormwood; and many men died of the waters, because they were made bitter.

¶ And the fourth angel sounded, and the third part of the sun was smitten, and the third part of the moon, and the third part of the stars; so as the third part of them was darkened, and the day shone not for a third part of it, and the night likewise.

¶ And I beheld, and heard an angel flying through the midst of heaven, saying with a loud voice, Woe, woe, woe, to the inhabiters of the earth by reason of the other voices of the trumpet of the three angels, which are yet to sound! Ch. 8:4-13

We are left in little doubt about the disastrous nature of this scenario: *and there were voices, and thunderings, and lightnings, and an earthquake...*-

and then – *and there followed hail and fire mingled with blood, and they were cast upon the earth: and the third part of trees was burnt up, and all green grass was burnt up.*

Right: The final trumpet sounds. Lincoln College Manuscript.

Opposite: **Hell,** by Dirck Bouts (1415-75), from the Musée des Beaux-Arts in Lille, France.

followed by – *and as it were a great mountain burning with fire was cast into the sea: and the third part of the sea became blood;*

And the third part of the creatures which were in the sea, and had life, died; and the third part of the ships were destroyed.

The picture drawn certainly appears to be about war, chaos and death, but strangely with an emphasis on the seas becoming blood. Why the seas? The oceans of earth here could symbolize the blood system. The health and strength of the human body is damaged by the blood borne disease that Nostradamus refers to often in his prophecies – possibly the plague of AIDS.

We hear also that a third part of the creatures in the seas died, a third part of the ships were destroyed, and a third part of the sea became blood. These images once again relate to mankind. The fish in the sea could be the humans on the planet, while the ships could symbolize commerce and the social and economic activities of man, while the blood filling a third part of the sea could be interpreted as the effect of AIDS and its associated diseases upon a third part of mankind. The prediction suggests that before AIDS and other major diseases are cured at their source, one third of humanity will be affected by them. This would therefore perhaps be part of the external apocalypse that we are in the midst of now. It is noticeable that in the past century the major diseases, far from becoming easier to cure, have in fact become greatly more sophisticated. It is as though the very curing of one disease leads directly to the appearance of another that is still more determined not to be cured. So, on a literal level, the horseman of pestilence will not cease to have his effect as long as mankind continues along its present route.

Another clue for the timing of this is the famous word "Wormwood" which refers to bitterness in the waters. The name of the Ukrainian town of Chernobyl, where a nuclear power station in the old Soviet Union first suffered the first melt-down and did so much damage to the areas of land around it and the people that lived there, translates into the herb named wormwood, thus giving us a possible direct connection with nuclear fallout and its results. Nuclear power would therefore be another aspect of the external apocalypse, the revelation of the twentieth century's end.

As we have seen earlier in the book, with the invention of the nuclear bomb mankind's capacity for self-destruction is greater than ever before.

And finally, in this doomy prediction we learn that it's not over yet.

And the fourth angel sounded, and the third part of the sun was smitten, and the third part of the moon, and the third part of the stars; so as the third part of them was darkened, and the day shone not for a third part of it, and the night likewise.

And I beheld, and heard an angel flying through the midst of heaven, saying with a loud voice, Woe, woe, woe, to the inhabitants of the earth by reason of the other voices of the trumpet of the three angels, which are yet to sound!

According to these verses we will face an overshadowing of the sun, moon and stars, and much of the day will have no light during the final apocalypse. This is a classic symptom of the presence of volcanic dust in the atmosphere which blocks out light, such as has happened during the biggest volcanic eruptions in our history – for example Krakatoa which erupted in 1883. But there is unlikely to be a volcanic eruption big enough to block out a third of

Right: After the Fire. **The Resurrection: Cookham** (detail), by Sir Stanley Spencer, in the Tate Gallery, London.

Previous pages, left: A funeral during the Chernobyl disaster in the Ukraine. The word *chernobyl* means "wormwood," the herb *Artemisia absinthium,* proverbial for its bitter taste. *Right:* The fourth trumpet sounds, from the Lincoln College Manuscript.

earth's exposure to the sun. A more likely scenario is the arrival of a massive meteorite that crashes into the earth and sends up masses of dust into the atmosphere. Given a big enough piece of spacerock, the predicted effect is entirely possible. There have, in fact, recently been a number of close misses from meteorites that have sped past earth, missing us by only a few hundred thousand miles – a close shave in astronomical terms.

So, if we believe these verses, we may expect a collision in the course of our apocalyptic transformation on earth.

And there is yet more to come, for the last lines predict further "untold" disasters. With the advent of the nuclear age, we are in uncharted waters. We have quantified the physical destruction our weapons can wreak, but the long-term genetic consequences of radiation poisoning are unknown.

The Last Oil Strike

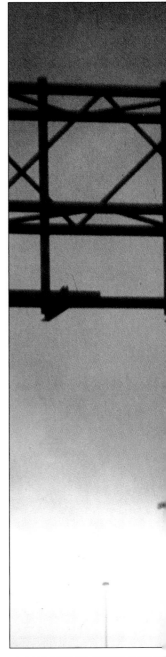

THE PROPHECIES OF REVELATION DO NOT NEGLECT THE MIDDLE EAST AS A part of the final physical apocalypse, and in chapter nine we learn of the "bottomless pit" that could lead to further wars over the possession of the world's most desired natural resource – oil. These wars, however, seem not to be fought as normal wars, but in the streets of the cities of the world.

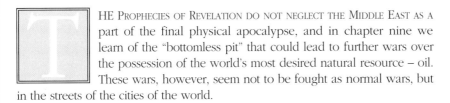

And the fifth angel sounded, and I saw a star fall from heaven unto the earth: and to him was given the key of the bottomless pit.

¶ And he opened the bottomless pit; and there arose a smoke out of the pit, as the smoke of a great furnace; and the sun and the air were darkened by reason of the smoke of the pit.

¶ And there came out of the smoke locusts upon the earth: and unto them was given power, as the scorpions of the earth have power.

¶ And it was commanded them that they should not hurt the grass of the earth, neither any green thing, neither any tree; but only those men which have not the seal of God in their foreheads.

¶ And to them it was given that they should not kill them, but that they should be tormented five months: and their torment was as the torment of a scorpion, when he striketh a man.

¶ And in those days shall men seek death, and shall not find it; and shall desire to die, and death shall flee from them.

¶ And the shapes of the locusts were like unto horses prepared unto battle; and on their heads were as it were crowns like gold, and their faces were as the faces of men.

¶ And they had hair as the hair of women, and their teeth were as the teeth of lions.

¶ And they had breastplates, as it were breastplates of iron; and the sound of their wings was as the sound of chariots of many horses running to battle.

¶ And they had tails like unto scorpions, and there were stings in their tails: and their power was to hurt men five months.

¶ And they had a king over them, which is the angel of the bottomless pit, whose name in the Hebrew tongue is Abaddon, but in the Greek tongue hath his name Apollyon.

¶ One woe is past; and, behold, there come two woes more hereafter. Ch. 9:1-12

Top: The fifth trumpet sounds, from the Lincoln College Manuscript.
Above: Devastation in the wake of the Siberian fireball of 1908, an example of a natural disaster which caused greater damage than either of the atomic bombs dropped on Japan. At the time, the catastrophe was seen as an act of God.
Opposite: Capping burning oil wells in Kuwait after the Gulf War.

Previous pages: Day into night – pall over Kuwait.

We can interpret this extraordinary piece of prophetic symbolism as beginning with what appears to be a fairly precise description of the depths of the earth from which oil is produced, and the result of the burning of it:

And he opened the bottomless pit; and there arose a smoke out of the pit, as the smoke of a great furnace; and the sun and the air were darkened by reason of the smoke of the pit.

Anyone who has visited an oil well site, or seen burning oil wells depicted on television, will be impressed by the apparent clarity of this description. And then:

And there came out of the smoke locusts upon the earth: and unto them was given power, as the scorpions of the earth have power.

Why locusts? The migratory locust was a symbol in the Old Testament and other ancient literature of voracity and destruction, because of its ability to devastate entire areas of land as it swept through eating everything. In Exodus a plague of locusts descends on Egypt as an affliction sent by God. In this verse it could represent the harmful effects of man's use of oil, both on himself and on his environment. Almost as though the drops of oil, like locusts, fly across the planet to touch everything – industrial plant, vehicles, cities, people – devastating and polluting in their wake.

And it was commanded them that they should not hurt the grass of the earth, neither any green thing, neither any tree; but only those men which have not the seal of God in their foreheads.

In this passage, the polluting force was denied the power to damage the countryside – *the grass of the earth, neither any green thing, neither any tree* – but granted the power to damage people who have no understanding, people without vision or belief. The phrase *those men that have not the seal of God in their foreheads* could represent the idea of having insight, self-knowledge, or God within. A seal was a symbol of ownership and the seal of God would have indicated "ownership" of God. The message here could therefore be that by the over-exploitation of the natural resources of the planet for economic gain, mankind has poisoned itself. By abandoning good sense and love of the environment in the pursuit of economic power through the use of these resources, we have lost much.

Right: The sixth trumpet sounds, Lincoln College Manuscript.
Opposite: Traffic jams in New York City – how much worse can it get?

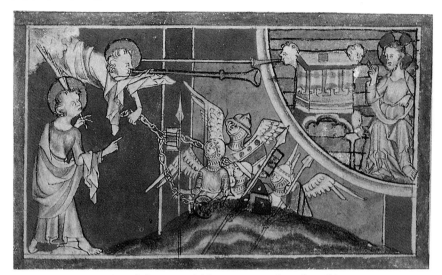

The verse that then follows could be interpreted as describing cars:

And the shapes of the locusts were like unto horses prepared unto battle; and on their heads were as it were crowns like gold, and their faces were as the faces of men ….

And they had breastplates, as it were breastplates of iron; and the sound of their wings was as the sound of chariots of many horses running to battle.

And they had tails like unto scorpions, and there were stings in their tails: and their power was to hurt men five months.

Given the biblical terms of reference, a clearer prophecy of the car would be hard to find. Our modern horseless chariots have helped cause pollution, congestion, the separating effect on the driver, the unconscious erosion of patience and the resulting aggression on the roads. This might, given the tendency in biblical language to exaggerate somewhat, be seen as a plague.

And finally we get the last clue to help confirm the location of our story – *And they had a king over them, which is the angel of the bottomless pit, whose name in the Hebrew tongue is Abaddon…*

Abaddon, or Abadan, as it is known today, represents the center of the oil industry in the Middle East. Situated in the province of Khuzestan, at the head of the Arabian Gulf, it is the terminus of Iran's major oil pipelines. It was severely damaged in the Gulf War.

The Hebrew word "abaddon" means hell, destruction, ruin, abyss – a place of absolute loss. Taken together, the "bottomless pit" – over-use of mineral resources – and the major problems of the motor vehicle in the latter years of the twentieth century, bring us to the "abyss" during the twenty-first century.

The Descent of Knowledge

And I saw another mighty angel come down from heaven, clothed with a cloud: and a rainbow was upon his head, and his face was as it were the sun, and his feet as pillars of fire:

¶ And he had in his hand a little book open: and he set his right foot upon the sea, and his left foot on the earth,

¶ And cried with a loud voice, as when a lion roareth: and when he had cried, seven thunders uttered their voices.

¶ And when the seven thunders had uttered their voices, I was about to write: and I heard a voice from heaven saying unto me, Seal up those things which the seven thunders uttered, and write them not.

¶ And the angel which I saw stand upon the sea and upon the earth lifted up his hand to heaven,

¶ And sware by him that liveth for ever and ever, who created heaven, and the things that therein are, and the earth, and the things that therein are, and the sea, and the things which are therein, that there should be time no longer:

¶ But in the days of the voice of the seventh angel, when he shall begin to sound, the mystery of God should be finished, as he hath declared to his servants the prophets.

¶ And the voice which I heard from heaven spake unto me again, and said, Go and take the little book which is open in the hand of the angel which standeth upon the sea and upon the earth.

¶ And I went unto the angel, and said unto him, Give me the little book. And he said unto me, Take it, and eat it up; and it shall make thy belly bitter, but it shall be in thy mouth sweet as honey.

¶ And I took the little book out of the angel's hand, and ate it up; and it was in my mouth sweet as honey: and as soon as I had eaten it, my belly was bitter.

¶ And he said unto me, Thou must prophesy again before many peoples, and nations, and tongues, and kings. Ch. 10:1-11

ONE OF THE MOST BIZARRE OF THE VERSES IN REVELATION IS THAT OF chapter ten.

As a piece of symbolism this chapter is more poetic and secretive than most. For its interpretation we must first take a look at some of the terms used.

Right: Rainbow – biblical ladder to God, or ascent into higher consciousness.

The first thing described is an angel wearing a cloud as a cloak, with a rainbow on his head, with the sun in his face and fire at his feet. This extraordinary angel carries a small book. So let's go back into the symbology of these items:

Clouds occupy the sky and have a mysterious veiling quality, as though they might be hiding something from us mortals on earth. To the ancients the clouds were the dwelling places of the gods, especially those that surrounded mountains such as Olympus.

The cloud therefore, wrapped about the angel, could represent mystery and remoteness – a kind of untouchable quality.

The rainbow was created, according to Talmudic tradition, on the evening of the sixth day of creation, connecting heaven and earth – almost like a ladder up to God. After the Flood, God put a rainbow in the skies as a sign of his compact with humanity. In medieval representations, He is shown seated upon a rainbow which often has only three primary colors. Each of these colors represents aspects of God's symbolic and biblical position in Christian belief, and we can find the connections between the colors and what they symbolize in many different sources, but for the sake of simplicity a reliable source is the *Herder Dictionary of Symbols*.

Blue is for the water of the flood and the color of the sky where God is said to dwell. Red symbolizes the final conflagration of the world – that is, the expected Christian apocalypse or Christ's passion – and green symbolizes the new world that will result from the apocalypse.

Having the sun in his face, the angel carries one of the most powerful symbols of all time – good, power, justice, victory and godliness. Fire beneath his feet signifies rebirth and purification. He offers us a little book to eat, which will taste like honey in the mouth, while in the belly it will be bitter.

As a prophecy this may appear highly controversial to anyone living in the twentieth century, for John could well be telling us that the sweet honey of spoken knowledge – the ability to express ourselves through education, learning, the application of our rational faculties – will ultimately only satisfy a very superficial aspect of human nature.

In the near future, as we reach out for the new world, science and technology will perhaps give way to a deeper and more profound wisdom and understanding, for learning is ultimately bitter to the unconscious (belly).

The Story of Woman

Top: The woman clothed with the sun brings forth her child.

Above: The woman flies to the desert, while the dragon makes war on her seed.

Opposite: **The Whore of Babylon,** by William Blake, 1809.

And she brought forth a man child, who was to rule all nations with a rod of iron: and her child was caught up unto God, and to his throne.

¶ And the woman fled into the wilderness, where she hath a place prepared of God, that they should feed her there a thousand two hundred and threescore days.

¶ And there was war in heaven: Michael and his angels fought against the dragon; and the dragon fought and his angels,

¶ And prevailed not; neither was their place found any more in heaven.

¶ And the great dragon was cast out, that old serpent, called the Devil, and Satan, which deceiveth the whole world: he was cast out into the earth, and his angels were cast out with him.

¶ And I heard a loud voice saying in heaven, Now is come salvation, and strength, and the kingdom of our God, and the power of his Christ: for the accuser of our brethren is cast down, which accused them before our God day and night.

¶ And they overcame him by the blood of the Lamb, and by the word of their testimony; and they loved not their lives unto the death.

¶ Therefore rejoice, ye heavens, and ye that dwell in them. Woe to the inhabiters of the earth and of the sea! for the devil is come down unto you, having great wrath, because he knoweth that he hath but a short time.

¶ And when the dragon saw that he was cast unto the earth, he persecuted the woman which brought forth the man child.

¶ And to the woman were given two wings of a great eagle, that she might fly into the wilderness, into her place, where she is nourished for a time, and times, and half a time, from the face of the serpent. Ch. 12:5-14

THE NEXT PART OF OUR JOURNEY THROUGH THE FUTURE CONCERNS THE evolution of woman. Verse five of Revelation chapter twelve can be interpreted as giving us a fascinating beginning to the prophetic story of the development of woman in history:

And she brought forth a man child, who was to rule all nations with a rod of iron: and her child was caught up unto God, and to his throne.

We are told that woman was, in effect, the channel through which man was born. From the very beginning of the Christian Church, man, as opposed to

woman, was seen as the earthly representative of God. Through Church and State, men ruled the world with a rod of iron, the iron being the base metal of alchemical transformation. The story thus begins with the use of religious and alchemical symbolism, the presumption being that ultimately human nature would turn from the rod of iron to the awakening of gold.

The story continues: *And the woman fled into the wilderness, where she hath a place prepared of God, that they should feed her there a thousand two hundred and threescore days*.

John appears to be telling us that woman took a "back seat" in the affairs of mankind, protected and nurtured by God, or his earthly representative, man, for a period of one thousand two hundred and sixty years. John frequently uses the astrological metaphor of "day" to imply longer periods of time.

If we take the "first day" to be the traditional year in which Christ was born (between AD 1 and 4), we find ourselves in the year 1260 or thereabouts. This could be seen as a period of European history when the male attitude to women underwent a profound change through the romantic era of chivalric and courtly love, and in which Arthurian legend and the myths and stories of the Holy Grail prevailed.

Looked at another way, using the Kabbalistic system of Gematria, by which numbers are given magical meaning, the year 1260 would be written in the Hebrew characters: *Taf, Taf, Taf, Samech* – תתתס.

These letters in Hebrew stand for the feminine qualities of: *Torah* (the scriptures) תורה, *Tevunah* (wisdom) תבונה, *To-eleth* (efficacy) תועלת, and *Sarbanuth* (stubbornness) סרבנות – deriving from the verb *Lesarev*, to refuse, and associated with the noun *Sarav*, meaning a thorn or briar. Thus from an interpretation using the Gematria we find feminine characteristics that can perhaps link the number 1260 to woman.

Thirteenth-century Europe saw the emergence of woman in the modern age from the darkness of repression – or, in religious terms, from her "protection" at the hands of men, the State and the Church.

And there was war in heaven: Michael and his angels fought against the dragon; and the dragon fought and his angels,

And prevailed not; neither was their place found any more in heaven.

And the great dragon was cast out, that old serpent, called the Devil, and Satan, which deceiveth the whole world: he was cast out into the earth, and his angels were cast out with him.

These lines seem to foretell the classical Arthurian stories of battles between the knights of chivalry and the devil (evil, the dragon), in which woman was idealized through art, literature, and poetry in works by authors such as Andreas Capellanus. In this elevated, albeit somewhat passive, role woman were at least for a while no longer considered simply as creatures needed for reproduction.

Woman was seen for much of history as the "alluring weaker vessel," and was believed to be a temptation to man. Her physical and emotional nature was felt to be subversive of the ascetic ideals of the male concept of the godhead, or man's connection with the divine.

This verse could be interpreted as meaning that once men began to be less in control, and women started on the road towards equality, there began a transformation in history from medieval to Renaissance understanding in Europe – towards the advent of female equality.

And I heard a loud voice saying in heaven, Now is come salvation, and strength, and the kingdom of our God, and the power of his Christ: for the accuser of our brethren is cast down, which accused them before our God day and night.

And they overcame him by the blood of the Lamb, and by the word of their testimony; and they loved not their lives unto the death.

Therefore rejoice, ye heavens, and ye that dwell in them. Woe to the inhabiters of the earth and of the sea! for the devil is come down unto you, having great wrath, because he knoweth that he hath but a short time.

And when the dragon saw that he was cast unto the earth, he persecuted the woman which brought forth the man child.

Opposite: An angel cries woe to the Earth for the dragon has come, Lincoln College Manuscript. Cast out of heaven, the defeated dragon persecutes emergent womankind, thus ending the age of chivalry.

Previous pages, right: **St. George and the Dragon,** by Paolo Uccello, *c.* 1397 – 1475. The legend that grew up around the third-century saint – describing how he rescued a maiden from a dragon at Silene in Libya, resulting in the baptism of thousands – was a late medieval addition.

Left: Golda Meir typifies the emergence of strong women in our times.

Above: Madonna, whose carefully cultivated image of self-sufficiency has made her a symbol of women's liberation.

Opposite: Scene from the Mass at the Epiphany Cathedral in Moscow in 1988.

The story then continues perhaps to tell us that the dragon (used in this context to denote the devil or unconsciousness), then took revenge on woman and persecuted her even more vehemently after her emergence. The dragon may be seen as the presence of unawareness within the psyche, as well as a stumbling block on the historical path of female evolution. In any event, if interpreted this way, the prophecy seems accurate, as following the "chivalric" period of medieval history in Europe, there came a disastrous period for women in which the natural cyclical magic of female energy was crushed. Church and secular authorities persecuted witchcraft and the feminine pre-Christian "nature" religion of Europe which survived in old-wives "superstitions" and natural folk remedies and wisdom.

We are next told:

And to the woman were given two wings of a great eagle, that she might fly into the wilderness, into her place, where she is nourished for a time, and times, and half a time, from the face of the serpent.

The *two wings of the great eagle* which were given to woman during this time of persecution, both echoes Exodus 19:4, in which God rescued Israel from its travails in Egypt, and represents the astrological sign of Scorpio in its higher form. As we have seen, Scorpio gives the power to persevere and be resolute in a time of difficulty, the power to transcend limitations and so go spiritually and psychologically higher or deeper. Scorpio also represents the secretive, often vengeful, aspect of human nature, which remains underground until the moment is right for a return to power. The wilderness into which the woman was to fly represents woman's exile in an ignorant world, and following the thirteenth century witchcraft was forced underground while men continued to maintain order.

We then read that this period of exile continued for *time, and times, and half a time, from the face of the serpent.* We may interpret this as indicating a period of two and a half centuries, bringing our next Revelation timing to approximately 1500, the High Renaissance.

Once again we can see this as a period when womankind took on a greater degree of strength, with positions of power being held by individuals such as Isabella of Castile (1451-1504), Lucrezia Borgia (1480-1519), Catherine de Medici (1519-89), Mary Queen of Scots (1516-58), Queen Elizabeth 1 of England (1533-1603) and many others.

Above: Renaissance women. Both
Mary Queen of Scots *(top)* and her
victorious rival, Elizabeth I of
England *(above),* embodied a
particular combination of strength
and femininity which shaped the
course of history.

Opposite: The Scarlet Woman, from a
Flemish Apocalypse, *c.* 1400, in the
Bibliothèque National in Paris.

The beginnings of a map of female independence starts to become clear.

We might imagine that the evident rise of womankind as a real force in the last years of the twentieth century would continue along lines that fit with our best hopes, but according to this interpretation of Revelation this may not be the case.

As before, we can best find a clear interpretation by taking one piece of the text at a time:

And there came one of the seven angels which had the seven vials, and talked with me, saying unto me, Come hither; I will shew unto thee the judgment of the great whore that sitteth upon many waters:

With whom the kings of the earth have committed fornication, and the inhabitants of the earth have been made drunk with the wine of her fornication. Ch. 17:1-2

John uses the symbology of the seven angels coming out of the heavens as a method of revealing different "sections" of his prophecies. This particular angel calls our attention to the presence of a symbolic prostitute – the "great whore."

As we have seen, Christianity absorbed the mythology and symbolism of earlier cultures into its own "format" of belief, taking parts of many, often ancient, understandings and adapting them to the "new" order. One of the most difficult aspects of the pagan past were the beliefs and practices revolving around the subject of sex. Christianity was (and still is) essentially sexually repressive, formulating concepts of Original Sin, fornication, and adultery in order to reinforce the values of marriage, fidelity, and the family unit. The imposition of new, Christian values proved to be difficult, for there were, as there are again, certain constant unresolved questions, such as the virgin birth, or the presence of characters such as Mary Magdelene, a prostitute. Within the Gnostic tradition she was known as the sacred harlot, embodying the goddess Sophia, who in turn was considered to be the powerful female part of God's soul. Again, within the early stories of Christianity, Simon Magus, a disciple of John the Baptist and one-time companion of Christ himself, traveled with a holy harlot named Helen, whom he worshipped as Sophia, the Gnostic Virgin of Light. The Gnostic gospels insisted that Jesus gave the mystic keys of the Kingdom of Heaven to Magdalena.

Christianity therefore had great problems in incorporating many of the ancient, pagan sexual beliefs, such as those surrounding fertility. In the centuries prior to the spread of Christianity, mankind understood the greater relevance of sexuality to life. Sexuality was seen not simply as an isolated activity that gave birth to more humans, but as a source of love, sensuousness, fecundity and the continued fertility of all life – plant and animal.

Opposite: The beauty of a
burgeoning woman has only
recently become an acceptable
image in Western society.
Below: Temple carvings at Khajuraho
in Madhya Pradesh, central India.

In this particular passage from Revelation we are confronted directly by this dichotomy – *I will shew unto thee the judgment of the great whore that sitteth upon many waters:*

With whom the kings of the earth have committed fornication, and the inhabitants of the earth have been made drunk with the wine of her fornication.

A female caste dating from ninth-century India called Devadasi (Sanskrit for "Handmaiden of God") included amongst their occupations that of holy prostitute within the temples of South India. The Devadasi signified fecundity within the Hindu understanding of sexuality, which differs radically from that of the West. The Hindus see orgasm as an analogy for the bliss of meditation, in which the self is extinguished in the godhead. The position of the Devadasi was considered one of great importance, and any tourist visiting India today will be left in no doubt as to the sexual dimension of Indian religion just by looking at the carvings on temple walls.

Reading the above lines from Revelation we might find the tone suitably judgmental, but in fact John is remarkably respectful of this "global" whore *who sitteth upon many waters,* and *With whom the kings of the earth have committed fornication,* and with whom *all and sundry have been made drunk with the wine of her fornication.* When John wrote Revelation, the pagan religions were still very much alive. In fact, it would be a thousand more years before Christianity ceased to be a persecuted faith in a world that still believed in many gods and goddesses. Anyone living at the time of John's writing would have had an understanding of pagan mythology, part of which were the ancient beliefs surrounding fertility goddesses.

In effect it can be interpreted that these lines allude to excesses of power and position and the way this power is used by men – *the kings of the earth.* So the story continues:

So he carried me away in the spirit into the wilderness: and I saw a woman sit upon a scarlet coloured beast, full of names of blasphemy, having seven heads and ten horns. Ch. 17:3.

Beasts are a common feature of Revelation, appearing in various forms throughout the text. They are perhaps amongst the most important of the symbols in the book. This particular beast has been mentioned before in another verse where, apart from the seven heads and ten horns, it is also shaped like a leopard with the feet of a bear and the mouth of a lion (Ch. 13:1-2).

The symbolism is significant, the leopard representing stealth, sensuousness, and swiftness, which in terms of psychological features gives us the characteristics of instinct and volatility, both seen as characteristics of essential femininity through their opposition to rationality.

The lion's mouth can be interpreted as an image of power and strength, but also with the idea of effective speech and articulation, which is significant in terms of the overall prophecy of women in positions of power. It may be relevant that the beast has no other attribute of the lion than its mouth; this would indicate, on the negative side, the characteristic of bombastic behavior. We can interpret this, then, as meaning that women will take on the behavior that men have displayed in the past.

The feet of a bear represent tenacity, anger and the enforcement of claims or possessions. Here again we can begin to form a picture from the text, and see a more powerful woman taking on the full roles that have hitherto been virtually the exclusive realm of men. The seven heads represent chaos; for each head carries horns which give authority to it, so that so much reason will make for conflict.

The picture begins to emerge of empowered womankind making all the mistakes of the past over again.

In real, on-the-ground terms, the newly empowered feminine aspect of society will create a number of fundamental changes.

For example, the rise of women in politics and industry may have a double impact on the generations of children that follow. Firstly, a predominance of real female energy may help reduce the likelihood of an increase in war. In addition, there may be a greater number of women with families who do not look after their children themselves but who leave this task either to the men or to babysitter.

Above: NATO Conference, London, 1990.
Margaret Thatcher represented a great step
forward for potential feminine power.

And the woman was arrayed in purple and scarlet colour, and decked with gold and precious stones and pearls, having a golden cup in her hand full of abominations and filthiness of her fornication:

¶ And upon her forehead was a name written, MYSTERY, BABYLON THE GREAT, THE MOTHER OF HARLOTS AND ABOMINATIONS OF THE EARTH.

¶ And I saw the woman drunken with the blood of the saints, and with the blood of the martyrs of Jesus: and when I saw her, I wondered with great admiration....

¶ And he saith unto me, The waters which thou sawest, where the whore sitteth, are peoples, and multitudes, and nations, and tongues.

¶ And the ten horns which thou sawest upon the beast, these shall hate the whore, and shall make her desolate and naked, and shall eat her flesh, and burn her with fire.

¶ For God hath put in their hearts to fulfil his will, and to agree, and give their kingdom unto the beast, until the words of God shall be fulfilled.

¶ And the woman which thou sawest is that great city, which reigneth over the kings of the earth. Ch. 17:4-18

Opposite: The power of woman has always been recognized in Hinduism. Here the goddess Kali, the Destroyer, makes love to Shiva's double corpse. Punjabi miniature, *c.* 1800, from the Gulbenkian Museum of Oriental Art in England.

Above: The marriage of Catherine de Medici to Henri II of France in 1533, when she was fourteen. She was to become the most powerful woman in France, wielding her influence over four reigns.

The last four verses in this chapter can be interpreted as revealing the woman to be in a position of considerable importance, perhaps as head of a new political and religious world order, or taking a leading part in the transformation of the Christian Churches, and giving women enormously greater power during the early years of the next century. It seems, however, that ultimately matters do not continue on an even keel, but that eventually poor decisions made while in positions of power cause woman to lose popularity. It would appear from this interpretation that she makes the same mistakes as men, and this may be an important factor in the equalization of men and women.

I N THE SECTION ON NUMERICS earlier, we mentioned the presence of various significant numbers in Revelation. Probably the most famous of these numbers, appearing as it does in many horror movies and works of fiction, is the number 666.

It has long been believed that this enigmatic numeric is the mark of the "Beast" signifying Satan, merged with the figure of the Antichrist. Beasts and devils have always preoccupied and fascinated us. It is part of our cultural conditioning to believe that there is not only an external manifestation of good, but also one of intense evil. But perhaps the number 666 and the extraordinary verses in Revelation concerned with the beast may have nothing whatever to do with evil.

During most periods in the past, where there has been a greater degree of suffering, war, and disease, the supposed presence of the beast – or sometimes the "Antichrist" – has assumed significance simply because of the pessimism that accompanies such ages. The twentieth century is just such an age. The Antichrist is expected at any time. We have already had one Antichrist, it seems, in the twentieth century and he, Hitler, helped create a holocaust of giant proportions. It is, we might imagine, only a matter of time before the next major upheaval – the apocalypse perhaps – is brought about by the next Antichrist in the form of a beast, or some other ghastly monster, who will no doubt bear the number 666, probably somewhere above the hair line, quite close to the horns.

We associate the word Christ with everything good and so an anti-Christ is of course evil, not simply against Christ.

If we take a look at the number 666 first, we find that within the numerological system of the Gematria it can be interpreted in a very different way from that popularly believed. In almost all non-Christian religious persuasions, the number six is not seen as bad. In the Kabbalah, the secret Jewish mystical tradition, it is regarded as the perfection of numbers. It relates to the six days of creation, and to the six letters of the name of God, the six orders of angels, the six heavenly bodies, and so on. In the Hebrew Gematria the number 666 does not signify anything particularly evil, but means a messiah – an individual who has a particular divine message to relate.

In Revelation the number 666 is given in the same breath, so to speak, as the beast, or apocalyptic animal. We are led to believe therefore, given our potent mythology of the devil, that the two are necessarily related and evil. But, as we have seen, the word apocalypse actually means a prophetic disclosure – a revealing of the truth. We might therefore, once again, try dropping our fearful

Opposite: Today the apocalyptic number 666 has lost it's power over us. Number 666 Fifth Avenue goes unnoticed.
Left: The second beast, with two horns like a lamb, coming up from the earth. Lincoln College Manuscript.

Previous pages: Part of a black magic ritual designed by Eliphas Levi in the nineteenth century, described in his book *Transcendental Magic* (1896).

preconceptions and consider the possibility that the apocalyptic "animal" numbered 666 might actually be human, and one who brings revelation – a messiah. Such a messiah could, of course, also be an "anti-Christ" insofar as he or she would not preach the old word of God, but a new "word." Thus, our new messiah could be a good messiah and still be an anti-Christ.

Within this verse of Revelation we are given a number of clues as to what kind of individual he, or she, might be:

He has: *seven heads and ten horns, and upon his horns ten crowns, and upon his heads the name of blasphemy.*

These qualities can be interpreted to signify that he will cause confusion in ordered society – seven heads and ten horns with ten crowns indicates a powerful capability to confuse order. Of course he will "blaspheme" because he will be against conventional Christianity.

Next we learn that: *the beast which I saw was like unto a leopard, and his feet were as the feet of a bear, and his mouth as the mouth of a lion: and the dragon gave him his power, and his seat, and great authority.*

This can be interpreted as a character study. In antiquity, and also in Roman mythology, the leopard was a symbol of wildness, aggression and power; in China it was also akin to the Moon, while the lion was akin to the Sun. According to ancient Greek mythology, the leopard was an attribute of the goddess Artemis and the god Dionysus, symbolizing strength and fertility, and as such was connected with the Bacchanalian cult of Dionysus. So our messiah is a powerfully "dangerous" character who perhaps has a tendency to behave in a very lively manner.

He is also lion-like in speech, in other words not holding back what he says; and in having the dragon give him power, he possesses primal powers – powers of nature that might not appeal to some sectors of orthodox religion.

Finally he has the feet of a bear, which symbolizes, through its ability to hibernate, the power of rebirth.

All in all, our messiah is an extraordinary character – wild, aggressive, powerful, eloquent, primal and an ancient spirit born many times.

And I saw one of his heads as it were wounded to death; and his deadly wound was healed: and all the world wondered after the beast.

The messiah evidently dies; but even after his death, his memory remains alive, and some bad is put right (healed), the world continuing to wonder at him.

We are next told a few things about what happens to this "anti-Christ" messiah:

...they worshipped the beast, saying, Who is like unto the beast? who is able to make war with him?

And there was given unto him a mouth speaking great things and blasphemies; and power was given unto him to continue forty and two months....

And it was given unto him to make war with the saints, and to overcome them: and power was given him over all kindreds, and tongues, and nations.

He appears to be world-famous and talked about, perhaps reported in the press. Once again we're told he has great oratorical powers. He lives forty-two years (days and years in the Bible are often switched). He attacks "saintliness," perhaps meaning that he opposes the values of the established Church, and he affects everyone, every tongue and nation.

In other words the messiah touches the whole world with his message – just as we might expect a messiah to do.

And then we learn still more about this messiah – that in fact there will be another messiah who will come after the first has died, and will, so to speak, bring the first again to public awareness.

And he exerciseth all the power of the first beast before him, and causeth the earth and them which dwell therein to worhip the first beast, whose deadly wound was healed.

Above: Revelation indicates that the Church of Rome will undergo a radical transformation.

Opposite: The sage Krishnamurti was plagued by followers who projected on to him their need for a Messiah.

And he doeth great wonders, so that he maketh fire come down from heaven on the earth in the sight of men,

And deceiveth them that dwell on the earth by the means of those miracles which he had power to do in the sight of the beast; saying to them that dwell on the earth, that they should make an image to the beast, which had the wound by a sword, and did live.

And he had power to give life unto the image of the beast, that the image of the beast should both speak, and cause that as many as would not worship the image of the beast should be killed.

This second messiah, it seems, performs miracles in the name of the first, encourages people to worship him, and promotes him as the only messiah for mankind, though there is deception and killing involved within this new religious "cult." It all sounds rather like a repetition of the advent of Jesus and the subsequent development of Christianity.

In summary, this verse can be interpreted as meaning that we will see a major change in Christianity, and the beginning of a new and powerful religion based on a messiah (or master, or guru) who has already lived on earth. Another individual will come in the near future and promote this master afresh.

The Christian Fall

And behold a great red dragon
having seven heads and ten horns.

And the temple of God was opened in heaven, and there was seen in his temple the ark of his testament: and there were lightnings, and voices, and thunderings, and an earthquake, and great hail.

¶ And there appeared a great wonder in heaven; a woman clothed with the sun, and the moon under her feet, and upon her head a crown of twelve stars:

¶ And she being with child cried, travailing in birth, and pained to be delivered.

¶ And there appeared another wonder in heaven; and behold a great red dragon, having seven heads and ten horns, and seven crowns upon his heads.

¶ And his tail drew the third part of the stars of heaven, and did cast them to the earth: and the dragon stood before the woman which was ready to be delivered, for to devour her child as soon as it was born.

¶ And she brought forth a man child, who was to rule all nations with a rod of iron: and her child was caught up unto God, and to his throne. Ch. 11:19; Ch. 12:1-5

THE MAIN FEATURE OF THIS PROPHECY CONCERNS THE SUN-CLOTHED Woman: *and her child was caught up unto God, and to his throne.* We are also told that during this period of our future: *and there were lightnings, and voices, and thunderings, and an earthquake, and great hail.*

The Sun-Clothed Woman can be interpreted as representing established Christian doctrine. Clothed with the sun, she is the force of life in the Church, and with the moon under her feet, she masters the emotions of chaos (the chaos that results from a lack of religious discipline). This is also a classical mythological symbol in the modern "Goddess movement" of creator and destroyer, and the twelve stars (planets) of the zodiac like a crown about her head give her all the facilities of thought and intellect.

Above: The sun-clothed woman bringing forth her child.
Right: The New Age has given rise to many playful
images. Cartomancer's house in Hollywood.

The taking of the child up into heaven once more can be seen as a symbolic representation of the end or transformation of the Church – having served its purpose it is then returned to the hands of God Himself. At this same time we will see (are already seeing) massive natural disasters, including floods and earthquakes.

In the overall tapestry that begins to be revealed we can see the external manifestation of the long-awaited apocalypse. The apocalypse is also reflected in the growing, inner transformation of spiritual awareness taking place at the end of the twentieth century, resulting from an increased interest in "alternative" religions and philosophies. We may also notice how the nations affected by the growth of a new religiousness, such as the United States and Europe, also, coincidentally, have to deal with the occurrence of famine, earthquake and other "natural" disasters. Although the shortage of grain, for example, arises in the future in areas such as Russia and remote parts of the United States, the areas affected by the resulting famine are exactly those also touched by the problems arising from the changes in the Christian Churches.

Right: Volcanic eruption, Mount St.
Helens, Washington State, 1980.
Opposite: Beacon of hope – the
Statue of Liberty, Ellis Island.

The Wrath and His Son

AFTER THIS LAST VERSE WE MOVE INTO A SERIES OF MAJOR retributions. The jealous God appears to take his revenge upon those who have left the Church and joined the new messiah. Or so it appears at first reading. But as always with biblical writing, there can be more beneath the surface. The Bible, and particularly the Book of Revelation, is full of "taken-for-granted" themes which appear in a very different light when we pay closer attention.

One such theme is that of divine retribution. The story behind chapters fourteen, fifteen, and sixteen appears at first glance to describe jealous, tantrum-like behavior on the part of God, directing his angels literally to destroy everyone who doesn't follow Him. This childish rage sounds, in fact, rather un-Godlike. Hardly appropriate behavior for an almighty archetype who supposedly created the universe. And if we turn up our microscope we may find that it is not quite like this.

Let us first consider a figure sitting in a cloud as the Son of Man, carrying a sickle in his hand.

And I looked, and behold a white cloud, and upon the cloud one sat like unto the Son of man, having on his head a golden crown, and in his hand a sharp sickle. Ch. 14:14.

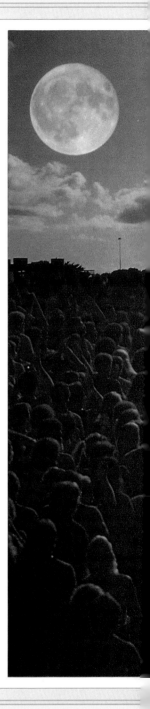

Left: The angels with the last plagues. Lincoln College Manuscript.

Right: Human harvest. The sickle held by the Son of Man is a metaphor for our power to make life fruitful. In working with nature, we renew the community and ourselves.

In the Book of Daniel (7:13), there is a similar reference to a "Son of man" who is given dominion and glory and who sits in judgment over humanity. According to traditional Christian belief this Son, the historical Jesus, is a representative of God's power who has the ability to decide our fate. Because of the conditioning of the Piscean age to accept the idea of an "outside" God, many of us may believe that we are being manipulated by some massively powerful, divine and external entity, who either condemns us to life imprisonment, or to death, because of our sins.

As children we are encouraged into positive and happy behavior, but very often once we become adult the Fairy Tale doesn't necessarily come true. We seem to be like reeds in the wind, at the whim of a fate over which we have no power or influence.

But the real truth is neither one nor the other. It is neither that we can live happily ever after, nor is it that we have to live in hell until we die. The underlying message that can be interpreted from the next verses of Revelation is precisely this. It is a message of the actual truth of life, on earth, here and now.

The Son of God can be seen as a metaphor for the unconscious individual power in each of us. The sickle that we carry is the power to make life fruitful.

The sickle symbolizes harvest which takes place each year. It is both a renewal of the land and its produce, and it signifies hope of renewal in us – our human rebirth. The message, indeed the prophecy, in these lines can be interpreted as being that we carry the power to make our lives work in our own hands, both as individuals and therefore in a sense as "gods" of the earth, and that we will inevitably do so. If we remember the seven letters to the seven churches, the same theme reverberates there – first the naivety of the physical, the childhood, then the shock of reality through self-reflection, followed by disillusionment and finally a rebirth to awakening – a Revelation, or apocalypse. Christians might see this as entering heaven after death, but a closer look suggests that this apocalypse results in heaven on earth during life.

Above: The harvest of the Earth *(top),* and the vintage of the Earth *(above),* from the Lincoln College Manuscript. *Opposite:* Tuscan vineyards – the view from San Miniato.

And another angel came out of the temple, crying with a loud voice to him that sat on the cloud, Thrust in thy sickle, and reap; for the time is come for thee to reap; for the harvest of the earth is ripe.

And he that sat on the cloud thrust in his sickle on the earth; and the earth was reaped. Ch. 14:15 – 16.

And sure enough the angel pops up, our guide to divine understanding, and tells us to reap the harvest – thrust the sickle into the earth and make the best of it. *The harvest of the earth is ripe* – there is plenty for everyone if we know how to make it flourish.

And another angel came out of the temple which is in heaven, he also having a sharp sickle.

And another angel came out from the altar, which had power over fire; and cried with a loud cry to him that had the sharp sickle, saying, Thrust in thy sharp sickle, and gather the clusters of the vine of the earth; for her grapes are fully ripe.

And the angel thrust in his sickle into the earth, and gathered the vine of the earth, and cast it into the great winepress of the wrath of God.

And the winepress was trodden without the city, and blood came out of the winepress, even unto the horse bridles, by the space of a thousand and six hundred furlongs. Ch. 14:17-20

The story continues with lyrical enthusiasm, with images of wine presses and ripe grapes, all symbols of richness and fruitfulness, intended to show how the world will be if we harvest it with care. And the fruit of all this reaping is placed into the winepress of the wrath of God or, put another way, the reaping of earth's riches needs to be done with religiousness – with all the juicy ingredients of godliness, meditation, love, self-reflection. It is then squeezed out of the winepress as blood – wine into blood, fruitfulness into that which circulates and feeds the human body, mind and spirit.

Christian interpretations of these texts speak of wrathful, bloody behavior, of death, anger, and end-of-world scenarios, the blood indicating suffering, pain and death. But perhaps God's will was not intended to be read like that. The words can, instead, be interpreted as compassionate and based upon the pagan values of renewal and rebirth. Husband the earth's resources, reap the land with good intentions, and ultimately you will feed yourselves.

And in other parts of Revelation, the same theme is echoed, with dire warnings of what can happen if we neglect our home-world.

The Great Famine

...And I beheld, and lo a black horse; and he that sat on him had a pair of balances in his hand.

¶ And I heard a voice in the midst of the four beasts say, A measure of wheat for a penny, and three measures of barley for a penny; and see thou hurt not the oil and the wine. Ch. 6:5-6

HE VERSES RELATING TO THE FOUR HORSEMEN HAVE ALREADY BEEN discussed in terms of the inner and outer apocalypse, but we can also take the same material and look at it specifically as a physical future scenario. Taken alone in this manner the words can be interpreted as a startling piece of prediction for a massive famine that forms part of the external apocalypse.

The black horse is associated with famine by the references to wheat, barley, oil, and wine, and in order to get a date for this famine we must look at the symbolism of the first line.

We are given a strong indication with the use of the horse and on the horse a man with a set of balances. This symbolism brings two cultures together that John would probably have been aware of – that of the Western science of astronomy/astrology, which then was one and the same, and the Eastern astronomy of China.

The horse has long had its place as a symbol in many cultures. Originally the horse was thought to be a chthonic creature, dwelling in or beneath the surface of the earth. It emerged from the chaotic underworld onto the earth's surface bringing various influences with it, in this case fire and water which were thought to be the forces of life and danger. Myths arose around the horse, therefore, that wherever its hooves struck the ground, springs of water would gush. Still today we use the concept of the flying horse to designate power and magic, and certain organizations around the world, including banks and petroleum companies, use the horse as a symbol of strength and sensitivity. It was also associated with both the moon and the realm of death, so that many ancient cultures would bury a man's horse with him to carry him through the afterlife.

Praying for rain in drought- and famine-stricken Mali in 1985.

Opposite and left: New York scrap, and a "bag lady." Greed, overproduction and waste in the First World create squalor amid plenty.

Within this verse we can find useful associations in astrology. In Chinese astrology we find the Year of the Horse, and in Western astrology Libra (the scales). In this one line, therefore, we are directed by the imagery to the Chinese Year of the Horse, and to the astrological sign of Libra by the presence of the balances in the rider's hands. The next Year of the Horse occurs during our era, a time when we are told by this verse that famine will represent such a threat to earth. This occurs between 27 January 2002 and 14 February 2003. During this time, according to this interpretation, we can expect the worst famine that earth has ever encountered, a famine that will affect a quarter of the world's population... *over the fourth part of the earth.* This famine, alongside the earthquakes and climatic changes mentioned earlier, represents the climax of several years of mismanagement of the world's resources.

The voice that was heard in the midst of the four beasts tells us: *A measure of wheat for a penny, and three measures of barley for a penny; and see thou hurt not the oil and the wine.* We learn from this that the areas to be afflicted by famine could be those that produce grain, not those that produce oil and wine. The main feature of the famine is that humanity has over-farmed grain-producing land, using intensive agricultural techniques. These eventually exhaust the land's capacity to produce enough grain to meet the increased demands of the last years of the twentieth century. The oil and wine producing areas of the world, predominantly Southern Europe and parts of the West Coast of the United States, together with Australia, are not *hurt* by the *sword, and with hunger, and with death, and with the beasts of the earth.*

Vitriolic Angels

And I saw another sign in heaven, great and marvelous, seven angels having the seven last plagues; for in them is filled up the wrath of God....

¶ And the seven angels came out of the temple, having the seven plagues, clothed in pure and white linen, and having their breasts girded with golden girdles.

¶ And one of the four beasts gave unto the seven angels seven golden vials full of the wrath of God, who liveth for ever and ever.

¶ And the temple was filled with smoke from the glory of God, and from his power; and no man was able to enter into the temple, till the seven plagues of the seven angels were fulfilled. Ch. 15:1-8

NOW WE COME TO THE MAGIC NUMBER SEVEN, AND FACE SEVEN DIFFERENT angels, each one with a task to perform.

And so we learn what happens when the seven vials are emptied, each one in the hands of a different angel:

ANGEL ONE – *And the first went, and poured out his vial upon the earth; and there fell a noisome and grievous sore upon the men which had the mark of the beast, and upon them which worshipped his image.* Ch. 16:2

ANGEL TWO – *And the second angel poured out his vial upon the sea; and it became as the blood of a dead man: and every living soul died in the sea.* Ch. 16:3

ANGEL THREE – *And the third angel poured out his vial upon the rivers and fountains of waters; and they became blood....* Ch. 16:4

ANGEL FOUR – *And the fourth angel poured out his vial upon the sun; and power was given unto him to scorch men with fire....*Ch. 16:8

ANGEL FIVE – *And the fifth angel poured out his vial upon the seat of the beast; and his kingdom was full of darkness; and they gnawed their tongues for pain,*

And blasphemed the God of heaven because of their pains and their sores, and repented not of their deeds. Ch. 16:10, 11

ANGEL SIX – *And the sixth angel poured out his vial upon the great river Euphrates; and the water thereof was dried up, that the way of the kings of the east might be prepared....* Ch. 16:12

ANGEL SEVEN – *And the seventh angel poured out his vial into the air; and there came a great voice out of the temple of heaven, from the throne, saying, It is done.* Ch. 16:17

Opposite: The Smaragdina tablet, an emblem representing all wisdom, with magical symbols. From an eighteenth-century mystical treatise. The Latin inscription refers to the curing of evil with the philosopher's stone.
Above: Ferment of the Sun and ferment of the Moon. An alchemical illustration from Elias Ashmoles' private copy of his book *Theatrum Chemicum Britannicum,* 1652. Ashmolean Museum, Oxford.

Previous pages: The angels are given the vials filled with the wrath of God. Lincoln College Manuscript.

These seven angels and their vials of poison are truly fascinating. Their position within Revelation coincides exactly with one of the fundamental formulas of alchemy. Once again, if we simply look at the story superficially, we might think that it is merely intended to instil the fear of hell and damnation into the hearts of men, but another interpretation can be more exciting than this.

And it all surrounds a word that we still use today. When we speak of something as being *vitriolic* we mean it has a bitterly malignant or poisonous quality, whether it be an actual chemical corrosive or the scathing effects of a caustic tongue. The seven angels with their seven vials could well be said to be *vitriolic,* for they are instructed, or so it seems, to cast the contents of the vials upon the earth for the apparent purpose of causing great suffering and destruction. During John's life, alchemy was one of the most important features of "science", and had been so since the ancient Egyptians began attempting to turn base metal into gold. Poison, as featured so predominantly in these verses of Revelation, was an essential feature of alchemy, expressed at that time as *vitriolic substance.*

But the word vitriol is also the acronym of an alchemical formula, which in the Latin has the first letters V.I.T.R.I.O.L. Note that there are also seven letters.

The formula in its full form is *Visita Inferiora Terrae Rectificando Invenies Occultum Lapidem,* meaning:

"Seek out the lower realms of the earth, perfect them, and thou wilt find the hidden stone." The stone is the alchemical Philosopher's Stone or *Lapis philosophorum,* which was believed to be the substance that acted as catalyst to change the base metal, iron, into enlightened gold within the medieval alchemical tradition.

The formula which we suggest arises out of these verses in Revelation is no more nor less than the ancient process of purifying base metals into gold, itself a metaphor for the search into the deepest recesses of the human consciousness – into one's own soul, to discover one's innermost essence. This is where the greatest secret on earth resides – the "hidden stone."

The seven angels with their seven vials can be interpreted as seeking out the lower realms of the earth and sea, and detoxifying them in order to begin the process of perfection, and to dig out the hidden human consciousness of mankind.

All that vitriol is merely a purification process to help mankind discover his own heart.

The final part of the chapter confirms the disastrous effects of this internal investigation:

And there were voices, and thunders, and lightnings; and there was a great earthquake, such as was not since men were upon the earth, so mighty an earthquake, and so great.

And the great city was divided into three parts, and the cities of the nations fell: and great Babylon came in remembrance before God, to give unto her the cup of the wine of the fierceness of his wrath.

And every island fled away, and the mountains were not found.

And there fell upon men a great hail out of heaven, every stone about the weight of a talent: and men blasphemed God because of the plague of the hail; for the plague thereof was exceeding great. Ch. 16:18-21

All this sounds very much like the world at the end of the twentieth century, and in fact this may be what the prediction is telling us – that in the last years of this millennium and the early years of the next, humanity could reach a state of critical mass, as more and more individuals reach an awakened state. And during the last approach towards that critical state, the external processes of the apocalypse – the natural convulsions of our planet, the divided and fallen cities, the coming of the Great Babylon, the sinking islands and vanishing mountains, the plagues of hail and unrepentant blasphemers – will all occur around us. As we read this book, much of it is already happening all over the world.

Twenty-First Century Babel

THIS PURIFICATION PROCESS THAT WE ARE TOLD WILL BE PART OF OUR NEAR future is already happening. The growing awareness of the need to cure pollution on earth is the beginning of a long and important story that will continue into the twenty-first century, as we find that our neglect of the planet is far, far worse than we had imagined. Revelation's prophecy that humanity will be purged of its poisons can be interpreted as a prediction of something positive and beneficial, which will result in a better world and a happier humanity. But then what can we expect?

And after these things I saw another angel come down from heaven, having great power; and the earth was lightened with his glory.

¶ And he cried mightily with a strong voice, saying, Babylon the great is fallen, is fallen, and is become the habitation of devils, and the hold of every foul spirit, and a cage of every unclean and hateful bird.

¶ For all nations have drunk of the wine of the wrath of her fornication, and the kings of the earth have committed fornication with her, and the merchants of the earth are waxed rich through the abundance of her delicacies.

¶ And I heard another voice from heaven, saying, Come out of her, my people, that ye be not partakers of her sins, and that ye receive not of her plagues.

¶ For her sins have reached unto heaven, and God hath remembered her iniquities.

¶ Reward her even as she rewarded you, and double unto her double according to her works: in the cup which she hath filled fill to her double.

¶ How much she hath glorified herself, and lived deliciously, so much torment and sorrow give her: for she saith in her heart, I sit a queen, and am no widow, and shall see no sorrow.

Car dump in Los Angeles, California – the
heaped-up aspirations of the consumer society.

Right: **The Tower of Babel,** by Pieter Brueghel the Elder, *c.* 1568, in the Kunsthistoriches Museum, Vienna.
Below: One of the twentieth-century Babels that collapsed.

¶ Therefore shall her plagues come in one day, death, and mourning, and famine; and she shall be utterly burned with fire: for strong is the Lord God who judgeth her.

¶ And the kings of the earth, who have committed fornication and lived deliciously with her, shall bewail her, and lament for her, when they shall see the smoke of her burning,

¶ Standing afar off for the fear of her torment, saying, Alas, alas, that great city Babylon, that mighty city! for in one hour is thy judgment come.

¶ And the merchants of the earth shall weep and mourn over her; for no man buyeth their merchandise any more:

¶ The merchandise of gold, and silver, and precious stones, and of pearls, and fine linen, and purple, and silk, and scarlet, and all thyine wood, and all manner vessels of ivory, and all manner vessels of most precious wood, and of brass, and iron, and marble,

¶ And cinnamon, and odors, and ointments, and frankincense, and wine, and oil, and fine flour, and wheat, and beasts, and sheep, and horses, and chariots, and slaves, and souls of men.

¶ And the fruits that thy soul lusted after are departed from thee, and all things which were dainty and goodly are departed from thee, and thou shalt find them no more at all.

¶ The merchants of these things, which were made rich by her, shall stand afar off for the fear of her torment, weeping and wailing,

¶ And saying, Alas, alas that great city, that was clothed in fine linen, and purple, and scarlet, and decked with gold, and precious stones, and pearls!

¶ For in one hour so great riches is come to nought. And every shipmaster, and all the company in ships, and sailors, and as many as trade by sea, stood afar off,

¶ And cried when they saw the smoke of her burning, saying, What city is like unto this great city!

¶ And they cast dust on their heads, and cried, weeping and wailing, saying, Alas, alas that great city, wherein were made rich all that had ships in the sea by reason of her costliness! for in one hour is she made desolate.

¶ Rejoice over her, thou heaven, and ye holy apostles and prophets; for God hath avenged you on her.

¶ And a mighty angel took up a stone like a great millstone, and cast it into the sea, saying, Thus with violence shall that great city Babylon be thrown down, and shall be found no more at all.

¶ And the voice of harpers, and musicians, and of pipers, and trumpeters, shall be heard no more at all in thee; and no craftsman, of whatsoever craft he be, shall be found any more in thee; and the sound of a millstone shall be heard no more at all in thee;

¶ And the light of a candle shall shine no more at all in thee; and the voice of the bridegroom and of the bride shall be heard no more at all in thee: for thy merchants were the great men of the earth; for by thy sorceries were all nations deceived.

¶ And in her was found the blood of prophets, and of saints, and of all that were slain upon the earth. Ch. 18:1-24

This "roll call" of the beneficiaries of trade, industry, and business can be seen as a prophecy about the future of commerce among nations and people.

The ancient city of Babylon on the Euphrates river is possibly used rhetorically, like many other things in Revelation, to symbolize something else.

Babylon was the capital of the Chaldean Empire. Its name in Hebrew, *Babel,* meant literally "portal of God." But over the centuries it became associated, especially within Christian literature, with the idea of confusion.

Because King Nebuchadnezzar destroyed the Temple and deported the Jews to Babylon, the city came to represent the opposite of the ideal – the antithesis of the heavenly Jerusalem.

Within these lines and elsewhere in Revelation, Babylon is a symbol of immoral, fraudulent and criminal dealings. The use of the word "fornication," we have seen, is not intended to mean sexual intercourse in this context, but rather dealings between individuals or groups who transact purely for monetary gain, without concern for godly values. In the *Compact Oxford English Dictionary* the word "fornication" used in a spiritual context is described as follows: "The forsaking of God for idols, idolatory – also spiritual fornication." The idols in this case being money and business dealing.

The detailed references here to all the items of trade – such as *fine linen, and purple, and scarlet, and decked with gold, and precious stones, and pearls –* narrows this extraordinary piece of prophecy down to world economics.

We can interpret this as meaning that we can expect a big clean-up of the global economic processes currently in use. That we are building a Tower of Babel that will only reach a certain point and then fail to function properly. At this point we may be forced to reconsider the entire business and industrial order of life on earth. In effect we will face the death of capitalism as it is today as a useful function of society.

We have already begun to see signs of this impending problem, with deep recession, fraudulent trading in various markets, collapsing stock markets, faltering insurance companies and bankrupted, criminally operated banks such as the Bank of Credit and Commerce International, which defrauded its clients out of hundreds of millions of dollars. Global economic growth during 1991 was literally stagnant, and in 1992 only rose by 1 percent.

We the public see only the most dramatic cases of fraud and economic breakdown that make the headlines. There are perhaps many more beneath the surface of public life that are not visible. As such immoral activities escalate, the global economy will begin to feel the result. Greater economic failure will occur, until, as the century closes, the scandals and problems will, once again, reach a critical mass and force governments to take a close look at the fundamental systems governing business and financial dealing all over the world. More concrete details of the form the new world's political arena will take are revealed in the final picture at the end of the book.

A Thousand Years of Peace

ONE OF THE MOST FAMOUS PREDICTIONS MADE BY THE SIXTEENTH-CENTURY prophet Nostradamus was that shortly after the beginning of the twenty-first century, mankind would embark on a thousand years of peace. We would largely see the end of war and major conflict for an entire millennium. Impossible though this may seem today, in the midst of war, and still not far from the memory of massive, global wars, the same prophecy is confirmed by John in Revelation. This lengthy peace, however, is predicated on the transformation of human nature through an internal and external apocalypse. Earth and its people will reach a warless world only if they awaken first – this is the message, loud and clear, of St. John's Revelation.

And I saw an angel come down from heaven, having the key of the bottomless pit and a great chain in his hand.

¶ And he laid hold on the dragon, that old serpent, which is the Devil, and Satan, and bound him a thousand years,

¶ And cast him into the bottomless pit, and shut him up, and set a seal upon him, that he should deceive the nations no more, till the thousand years should be fulfilled: and after that he must be loosed a little season. Ch. 20:1-3

And following this thousand years of peace, comes war and conflict once more!

And when the thousand years are expired, Satan shall be loosed out of his prison,

¶ And shall go out to deceive the nations which are in the four quarters of the earth, Gog and Magog, to gather them together to battle: the number of whom is as the sand of the sea.

¶ And they went up on the breadth of the earth, and compassed the camp of the saints about, and the beloved city: and fire came down from God out of heaven, and devoured them.

¶ And the devil that deceived them was cast into the lake of fire and brimstone, where the beast and the false prophet are, and shall be tormented day and night for ever and ever.

¶ And I saw a great white throne, and him that sat on it, from whose face the earth and the heaven fled away; and there was found no place for them.

¶ And I saw the dead, small and great, stand before God; and the books were opened: and another book was opened, which is the book of life: and the dead were judged out of those things which were written in the books, according to their works.

¶ And the sea gave up the dead which were in it; and death and hell delivered up the
dead which were in them: and they were judged every man according to their works.
¶ And death and hell were cast into the lake of fire. This is the second death.
¶ And whosoever was not found written in the book of life was cast into the lake of
fire. Ch. 20:7-15

And so the story of mankind continues, from mountain top to valley and back
again. A thousand years is, for most of us, an unimaginable time-span. And then,
to add to this, continuous peace is still harder to imagine, for us, who have lived
through the warring madness of the twentieth century. A millennium of peace
will mean fundamental changes in every aspect of life, but, if we follow the
processes outlined in Revelation, there are many elements that are needed to
bring about this condition. We will not simply stop fighting amongst ourselves
from one day to the next. From the seven letters to the Asian churches we have
learned of the transformation that could be expected, in which we will grow
through an evolution of understanding of ourselves into a greater wisdom and
eventual awakening. With the greater presence of women as a source of
inspiration and power, further changes will be felt which may take humanity
away from conflict. And as the internal apocalypse detoxifies our spiritual
natures, so the outside world will be refreshed, and ultimately we may reach a
state of inner peace which will influence the way that we relate both to our
surroundings and to each other. Perhaps then, the thousand years of peace will
be possible.

But then, in the last verses of this part of Revelation, we learn that following
the millennium of peace the "devil" will be released to bring more agonies.
"Satan," the biblical metaphor for all things evil, will return. The saints will be
besieged, the devil will join with false prophets and then be cast into the "fiery
lake" for eternal damnation – all good apocalyptic expression. And finally, the
"Last Judgment" will come. All this we can anticipate for the thirty-first century,
the second half of the Age of Aquarius.

Opposite: **The Last Judgement,** by
William Blake, 1808. In Blake's
vision, Christ is seated on the
Throne of Judgement in heaven.
The Earth beneath is convulsed with
the labors of the Resurrection. The
seven-headed Dragon is chained by
angels in the caverns below. Above,
on the Earth's surface, the Harlot is
seized by angels. On Christ's right
(our left), the Just arise, on his left
the Wicked fall.

The City of Gold
and Precious Stones

S THE CLOSING CURTAIN ON THE STORIES OF REVELATION COMES DOWN, we are given a final drawing of the heaven we can expect. This is the New Jerusalem, the "Heaven" that all Christians believe in – the promise of Jesus that after life there is a better place to go. Perhaps there is, but surely it seems a much better idea that the New World in the future will come about during life, not after it.

And I saw a new heaven and a new earth: for the first heaven and the first earth were passed away; and there was no more sea.

¶ And I John saw the holy city, new Jerusalem, coming down from God out of heaven, prepared as a bride adorned for her husband.

¶ And I heard a great voice out of heaven saying, Behold, the tabernacle of God is with men, and he will dwell with them, and they shall be his people, and God himself shall be with them, and be their God.

¶ And God shall wipe away all tears from their eyes; and there shall be no more death, neither sorrow, nor crying, neither shall there be any more pain: for the former things are passed away.

¶ And he that sat upon the throne said, Behold, I make all things new. And he said unto me, Write: for these words are true and faithful.

¶ And he said unto me, It is done. I am Alpha and Omega, the beginning and the end. I will give unto him that is athirst of the fountain of the water of life freely.

¶ He that overcometh shall inherit all things; and I will be his God, and he shall be my son.

¶ But the fearful, and unbelieving, and the abominable, and murderers, and whoremongers, and sorcerers, and idolaters, and all liars, shall have their part in the lake which burneth with fire and brimstone: which is the second death.

¶ And there came unto me one of the seven angels which had the seven vials full of the seven last plagues, and talked with me, saying, Come hither, I will shew thee the bride, the Lamb's wife.

¶ And he carried me away in the spirit to a great and high mountain, and shewed me that great city, the holy Jerusalem, descending out of heaven from God,

¶ Having the glory of God: and her light was like unto a stone most precious, even like a jasper stone, clear as crystal;

¶ And had a wall great and high, and had twelve gates, and at the gates twelve angels, and names written thereon, which are the names of the twelve tribes of the children of Israel:

¶ On the east three gates; on the north three gates; on the south three gates; and on the west three gates.

¶ And the wall of the city had twelve foundations, and in them the names of the twelve apostles of the Lamb.

¶ And he that talked with me had a golden reed to measure the city, and the gates thereof, and the wall thereof.

¶ And the city lieth foursquare, and the length is as large as the breadth: and he measured the city with the reed, twelve thousand furlongs. The length and the breadth and the height of it are equal.

¶ And he measured the wall thereof, an hundred and forty and four cubits, according to the measure of a man, that is, of the angel.

¶ And the building of the wall of it was of jasper: and the city was pure gold, like unto clear glass.

¶ And the foundations of the wall of the city were garnished with all manner of precious stones. The first foundation was jasper; the second, sapphire; the third, a chalcedony; the fourth, an emerald;

¶ The fifth, sardonyx; the sixth, sardius; the seventh, chrysolite; the eighth, beryl; the ninth, a topaz; the tenth, a chrysoprasus; the eleventh, a jacinth; the twelfth, an amethyst.

¶ And the twelve gates were twelve pearls; every several gate was of one pearl: and the street of the city was pure gold, as it were transparent glass.

¶ And I saw no temple therein: for the Lord God Almighty and the Lamb are the temple of it.

¶ And the city had no need of the sun, neither of the moon, to shine in it: for the glory of God did lighten it, and the Lamb is the light thereof.

¶ And the nations of them which are saved shall walk in the light of it: and the kings of the earth do bring their glory and honour into it.

¶ And the gates of it shall not be shut at all by day: for there shall be no night there.

¶ And they shall bring the glory and honour of the nations into it.

¶ And there shall in no wise enter into it any thing that defileth, neither whatsoever worketh abomination, or maketh a lie: but they which are written in the Lamb's book of life. Ch. 21:1-27

¶ And he shewed me a pure river of water of life, clear as crystal, proceeding out of the throne of God and of the Lamb.

¶ In the midst of the street of it, and on either side of the river, was there the tree of life, which bare twelve manner of fruits, and yielded her fruit every month: and the leaves of the tree were for the healing of the nations.

Opposite: The New Heaven and the New Earth with the Holy City. Lincoln College Manuscript.

Previous pages: Sunset from the summit of Snowdon, North Wales.

Above: God judges the dead.
Opposite: St. John is forbidden to kneel before the angel sent by God. Both from the Lincoln College Manuscript.

¶ And there shall be no more curse: but the throne of God and of the Lamb shall be in it; and his servants shall serve him:

¶ And they shall see his face; and his name shall be in their foreheads.

¶ And there shall be no night there; and they need no candle, neither light of the sun; for the Lord God giveth them light: and they shall reign for ever and ever.

¶ And he said unto me, These sayings are faithful and true: and the Lord God of the holy prophets sent his angel to shew unto his servants the things which must shortly be done.

¶ Behold, I come quickly: blessed is he that keepeth the sayings of the prophecy of this book.

¶ And I John saw these things, and heard them. And when I had heard and seen, I fell down to worship before the feet of the angel which shewed me these things.

¶ Then saith he unto me, See thou do it not: for I am thy fellowservant, and of thy brethren the prophets, and of them which keep the sayings of this book: worship God.

¶ And he saith unto me, Seal not the sayings of the prophecy of this book: for the time is at hand.

¶ He that is unjust, let him be unjust still: and he which is filthy, let him be filthy still: and he that is righteous, let him be righteous still: and he that is holy, let him be holy still.

¶ And, behold, I come quickly; and my reward is with me, to give every man according as his work shall be.

¶ I am Alpha and Omega, the beginning and the end, the first and the last.

¶ Blessed are they that do his commandments, that they may have right to the tree of life, and may enter in through the gates into the city.

¶ For without are dogs, and sorcerers, and whoremongers, and murderers, and idolaters, and whosoever loveth and maketh a lie.

¶ I Jesus have sent mine angel to testify unto you these things in the churches. I am the root and the offspring of David, and the bright and morning star.

¶ And the Spirit and the bride say, Come. And let him that heareth say, Come. And let him that is athirst come. And whosoever will, let him take the water of life freely.

¶ For I testify unto every man that heareth the words of the prophecy of this book, If any man shall add unto these things, God shall add unto him the plagues that are written in this book:

¶ And if any man shall take away from the words of the book of this prophecy, God shall take away his part out of the book of life, and out of the holy city, and from the things which are written in this book.

¶ He which testifieth these things saith, Surely I come quickly. Amen. Even so, come Lord Jesus.

¶ The grace of our Lord Jesus Christ be with you all. Amen. Ch. 21:1-21

In order to attempt to create something concrete from this extraordinary and ancient ideal, we must first, as always, take a look at ourselves.

Recovering Bliss

ONE OF THE FUNDAMENTAL PROBLEMS OF MODERN SOCIETY — which, when we look more closely at our potential new Eden, we will find is in direct contrast to it – is the overwhelming presence of negativity and disbelief. Even idealism has become something of a mistrusted concept, for the idea that experience leads to pain is still predominant. Cynicism may be the result of experience, but not all experience need lead to cynicism.

Within this interpretation of the Book of Revelation, probably the most important single prediction is the greater presence of women as a source of power in the world. The presence of an imbalance of male energy is fundamental to our problems.

The second vital element of the future is the return of religiousness. By religiousness we do not mean religion. During the next decades we will perhaps start to see the transformation of organized social religions. Human nature needs religiousness as much as it needs love, for true spirituality is a return to magic. And this is not the magic of occultism, but the magic of inspiration and divinity that is derived from intuition. With the predominance of reductionism and cynicism, this instinctual magic has gone underground somewhat. Profound religiousness entails a willingness to sample inner divinity, to listen to our God inside ourselves, and know that we are each of us the central source of love and enlightenment – that life gives birth to itself simply out of an intense passion for more life, and that each individual is simply an opportunity for greater human awakening. That, in truth, is all there is to it.

Given these two vital changes in our future – the tilting of the balance towards female power, and the return to an individual self-regulating motivation – the new Eden can begin to develop. And this has little to do with "belief" in the old Piscean sense of the word, for with this kind of fixed belief comes problems; the moment we believe in a defined god he dies – made stagnant through being fixed. The new Eden that is reflected in the vision of Jesus is alive, changing and perfectible, as we are. And in order to allow it to happen we must first recover bliss, those moments of pure simple joy that we associate with, perhaps, the birth of a child or first falling in love, moments that we faintly remember feeling when we were young children. This bliss, when allowed expression within our fundamental natures, is what fires the ideal. We have only forgotten and been encouraged to forget it by a society that has needed our continued anxiety to fuel its progress. The new world does not need this anxiety, it needs our individual magic. Then it can perhaps happen.

Opposite: New York skyline.
Above: Meditation puts us in touch with the wellsprings of our being.

Eden

SO TO FIND THE ESSENTIAL ELEMENTS OF OUR FUTURE EDEN LET US TAKE the last two chapters of the Bible and find what they mean to us – hopefully with our hearts open.

Verse three begins with the most important of all the qualifications for joy:

And I heard a great voice out of heaven saying, Behold, the tabernacle of God is with men, and he will dwell with them, and they shall be his people, and God himself shall be with them, and be their God. Ch. 21:3

The essence of human joy is to be with God. This does not imply that God is elsewhere – somewhere up above the clouds – but *"with men* [and women]". As if to emphasize the point the verse repeats the idea several times – he will dwell with them, and they shall be his people, and God himself shall be with them, and be their God. God lives in us, not outside us. Here is the root of Eden.

And next:

And God shall wipe away all tears from their eyes; and there shall be no more death, neither sorrow, nor crying, neither shall there be any more pain: for the former things are passed away. Ch. 21:4

Left: Sufis whirling in Moscow.
Previous pages: Llyn yr Adar,
Beddgelert, North Wales.

It is not that this God – out there as an external power – shall wipe away all tears from their eyes, but rather that the presence of godliness within each of us brings blissfulness and joy. The godhead kills troubles. And there shall be no more death, means not that we will somehow become physically immortal, but that death and life become one and the same. In the presence of magic and intuition, the division between life in the body and the spirit is the only thing that dies. Death ceases to be a burden, and fear disappears. With the disappearance of fear comes clarity and *neither sorrow, nor crying, neither shall there be any more pain: for the former things are passed away.*

Our new Eden contains a transformation of human understanding, not the presence of a second-come messiah who gives us all the answers. We have to find the answers ourselves. The presence of a messiah is not something new – there have been numerous messiahs and enlightened individuals in our past and we have largely ignored them. Messiahs will come in plenty also in the future, but they are not themselves the answer of our new Eden. They simply help it along, as Jesus did.

So our Eden will be founded on the deeply felt divinity of natural religiousness – the concern for the heart rather than the mind. This will, together with the greater presence of women in positions of power, lead to a change in the patterns of childbirth. A greater understanding of children's needs will reinforce the sense of inner well-being so often denied a child. A child with less fear becomes an adult with greater inner stability.

The outer manifestations of this development could be seen as self-regulated government and law. The best possible "engine" for a benevolent and concerned communal democracy could perhaps be an oligarchic administration similar at least in its basic system to that already functioning within the Swiss federation.

Next we are given a simple, basic set of qualities for human happiness:

But the fearful, and unbelieving, and the abominable, and murderers, and whoremongers, and sorcerers, and idolaters, and all liars, shall have their part in the lake which burneth with fire and brimstone: which is the second death. Ch. 21:8

It could be interpreted, therefore, that John tells us that in our new society we should:

1. abhor fear,
2. keep faith with ourselves (belief),
3. behave with good hearts (self-respect),
4. never kill, for no one has the right to take another life,
5. make love only with respect,
6. avoid the dark side of magic,
7. worship all life and not mutated versions of it,
8. avoid lying.

This last quality is perhaps meant to imply lying to ourselves, falsifying our emotional needs and our relationships with others.

Next we find the first mention of the most important basis of the new world – that it is essentially feminine:

> And there came unto me one of the seven angels which had the seven vials full of the seven last plagues, and talked with me, saying, Come hither, I will shew thee the bride, the Lamb's wife.
>
> ¶ And he carried me away in the spirit to a great and high mountain, and shewed me that great city, the holy Jerusalem, descending out of heaven from God,
>
> ¶ Having the glory of God: and her light was like unto a stone most precious, even like a jasper stone, clear as crystal; Ch. 21:9-11

The city of perfection is the "Lamb's bride." The Lamb, throughout Revelation, can be interpreted as a symbol of peace and love, and the bride of peace and love is woman. In our new world it is woman that sustains the Lamb of God – the Lamb being a symbol of the capability of humanity to be either peaceful or not.

And the city glowed with a precious jasper stone, clear as crystal – symbol, as we have learned, of birth and fertility because of its quality of appearing to reproduce itself when broken. The fractured jasper stone creates new light and new precious stones out of the fracturing, and so represents the power to give birth. Mention of crystal also implies clarity of vision.

We also learn something of the architecture of the city, with its high walls and twelve gates – symbolizing the twelve signs of the zodiac and twelve months of the year. The twelve angels, one at each gate, symbolize a recognition of the spirit world and its power to aid us in our physical lifetimes. To press the point home, the city has twelve foundations, each one imbued with the qualities of the original disciples of Jesus – wise men and true. The dimensions of the city are

Energy and purity - two essential elements of the New Eden.

given as "foursquare," and twelve thousand furlongs – length, breadth, and height the same – its power and long life encompassing land and sky. The wall in total measures one hundred and forty-four cubits round.

The measuring unit of the cubit was commonly used in ancient cultures. Also known as the "covid," or a "kus," it probably originated in Egypt around 3000 BC, becoming ubiquitous throughout the ancient world thereafter. One cubit is the approximate equivalent of 18 – 20 inches or 45.7 – 52.4 centimeters. This measurement was based on the length of the arm from the elbow to the extended fingertips, and could be subdivided into around 28 "digits," with 4 digits equaling a palm, and 5 digits a full hand. Twelve digits was known as a "small span" and 14 a "large span." Sixteen digits was a "t'ser," and 20 digits a small cubit. A similar cubit existed in the Rome of Jesus' time, and was also used by the Hebrew people.

Our city wall therefore measures a total of 80 yards in height. And the city is 1,500 miles square – far bigger than any city currently standing – somewhere near the size of an "urban corridor" that could run from, say, Washington, through New York to Baltimore.

The implications of this are that this great city will ultimately rule the world, providing the seat of a global government.

And so we turn to the building materials of the new Eden:

And the building of the wall of it was of jasper: and the city was pure gold, like unto clear glass.

¶ And the foundations of the wall of the city were garnished with all manner of precious stones. The first foundation was jasper; the second, sapphire; the third, a chalcedony; the fourth, an emerald;

¶ The fifth, sardonyx; the sixth, sardius; the seventh, chrysolite; the eighth, beryl; the ninth, a topaz; the tenth, a chrysoprasus; the eleventh, a jacinth; the twelfth, an amethyst.

¶ And the twelve gates were twelve pearls; every several gate was of one pearl: and the street of the city was pure gold, as it were transparent glass. Ch. 21: 18-21

Once again we find jasper and gold, the latter having given rise to the idea of heaven being paved with gold. The jasper we have already spoken of; the gold represents the purity of enlightenment of the people inhabiting the city. There is, of course, no connection with wealth in monetary terms.

Each foundation is then awarded a different precious or semi-precious stone as its make-up:

Jasper – clarity, and rebirth; Sapphire – healing and a reflection of heavenly protection; Chalcedony (Agate) – healing, aphrodisiac, concentration and

The Tree of Life, a modern batik in the Church of St. Botolph, City of London.

meditation; Emerald – fertility, the moon and spring; Sardonyx (a form of quartz that was once considered more precious than gold or silver) also known as Onyx; Sardius (derived also from quartz formations found in Sardis, the ancient capital of Lydia) also known as Carnelian; Chrysolite, Beryl, Topaz, Chrysoprasus, Jacinth, and Amethyst all bring elements of humility. The twelve gates are twelve pearls, symbolizing once again the feminine qualities, as well as immortality, love and beauty.

And next we find:

And I saw no temple therein; for the Lord God Almighty and the Lamb are the temple of it. Ch. 21:22

This can mean that there is no need for churches because churches symbolize the outer, organized religions, and this will be a thing of the past. The godliness of the new Eden will be within the temple of each individual.

As we move on to the last chapter of Revelation, we find more characteristics of our future, ideal world.

And he shewed me a pure river of water of life, clear as crystal, proceeding out of the throne of God and of the Lamb. Ch. 22:1

This river, flowing from the throne of God and the Lamb, was, during the Middle Ages, believed to be the source of all the oceans of the world – known as the River Ocean, flowing out of heaven and surrounding the earth like an island. Rivers generally, in symbolic terms, represent fertility and the transitory nature of life, also perpetual self-renewal. In Buddhism and Hinduism the flowing of rivers into the sea symbolizes the dissolving of the ego into Nirvana.

In the midst of the street of it, and on either side of the river, was there the tree of life, which bare twelve manner of fruits, and yielded her fruit every month: and the leaves of the tree were for the healing of the nations. Ch. 22:2

And this river flows through the center of the city with the tree of life straddling either side to heal those living on either bank. Sadly today, in most cities of the world, the rivers and trees are so polluted that their healing properties are impaired and neglected – it is the rivers and nature that need healing, and perhaps we can be the ones do it.

And there shall be no more curse: but the throne of God and of the Lamb shall be in it; and his servants shall serve him:

And they shall see his face; and his name shall be in their foreheads. Ch. 22:3-4

Here we find the contrast to the mark of the beast on the foreheads of those who might consider false messiahs. In this case we have the mark of the Lamb. This gives us an equivalent of an Eastern spiritual concept known as "killing the master on the road." Disciples who sit at the feet of the master and surrender to his or her teachings are eventually supposed to find their own way. But in order to become god within oneself, the master must metaphorically be killed, or his influence will hamper the disciple's progress. In this verse John perhaps is telling us that ultimately only our own qualities of purity and self-regulation will suffice – the inner conscience and wisdom of the so-called witness.

And next, among the qualities for the governing of this future world, is justice:

He that is unjust, let him be unjust still: and he which is filthy, let him be filthy still: and he that is righteous, let him be righteous still: and he that is holy, let him be holy still.

And, behold, I come quickly; and my reward is with me, to give every man according as his work shall be. Ch. 22:11-12

The ultimate form of justice is the acceptance of each individual for what he or she is. This is true compassion. Right and wrong cease to exist as judgments, because they both exist within each of us as two sides of a coin. Only what is practical and fruitful will occur in the city. People who have achieved full self-awareness will find new ways of living together. The changed harmonious relationships that flow from this state ensure the absence of crime. Justice will come from within.

This remarkable vision of great poetic power is the last word of the Bible. It even mirrors the first book, Genesis,

Below: **The Adoration of the Lamb,** by Jan van Eyck, 1432. Central panel of the Ghent Altarpiece, in the Cathedral of St. Bavon, Ghent.

Previous pages: **Architecture: its Natural Model,** a watercolor by Joseph Gandy, 1838, in Sir John Soane's Museum, London.

insofar as it contains reference to the Tree of Life. Here, in this new Eden, we have everything that is the flowering of mankind, using every symbolic item to describe the place. This new Eden, symbol of mankind's enlightenment – today perhaps seeming an impossible dream – will, according to this interpretation of Revelation and according also to many prophets from our past, become a reality in our future. The New Jerusalem is not a physical city, but the perfected state of the world endangered by the flowering of human conciousness – in all senses a return to primal innocence and Paradise Regained.

This attempt at interpreting the Book of Revelation in a positive light, perhaps gives us one conclusion, a conclusion that appears only if we come closer to the words and symbols hidden "between the lines." John and the men and women closest to Jesus, and who gave birth to what would much later become Christianity, carried a positive, apocalyptic message – that humanity is traveling on an essentially beautiful and positive path towards enlightened intelligent consciousness. As part of that potentiality, along the way, there are stumbling blocks, there is the suffering that brings understanding, and there is the presence of an inner godliness that we all have access to if we begin to look in that direction.

Once we turn inwards and look freshly at ourselves, then the external landscapes also brighten, and with our newfound sight, we can look joyfully at the world we inhabit, so that that world will also brighten and become joyful. It is up to each of us.

INDEX
BIBLIOGRAPHY
ACKNOWLEDGMENTS

SELECT BIBLIOGRAPHY

Steiner, Rudolf. **The Apocalypse of St. John.** New York: Rudolf Steiner Publishing Co., 1943. London: Rudolf Steiner Press, 1977.

Heidenreich, Alfred. **The Book of Revelation.** Edinburgh: Floris Books, 1977.

Fox, Robin Lane. **The Unauthorized Version - Truth and Fiction in the Bible.** London: Penguin Books, 1991; New York: Viking, 1992.

Thiering, Barbara. **Jesus The Man.** New York: Doubleday, 1992.

Barnwell, F. Aster. **Meditations on the Apocalypse - A Psycho-Spiritual Perspective on the Book of Revelation.** Shaftesbury, Dorset: Element Books 1992.

Johnson, Paul. **A History of Christianity.** London: Weidenfeld & Nicolson, 1976. London: Penguin Books, 1990.

Eliade, Mircea. **From Primitives to Zen.** London: William Collins, 1967.

Lorie, Peter. **Nostradamus - The Millennium and Beyond.** New York: Simon & Schuster, 1993.

Armstrong, Karen. **A History of God.** London: William Heinemann Ltd, 1993.

ACKNOWLEDGMENTS

Special thanks are owed to Dr. Colin McEvedy, author of the Penguin Historical Atlases, for his help in providing information, statistics, maps and charts related to the section on the Four Horsemen of the Apocalypse.

This book is dedicated to Osho.

PICTURE CREDITS

St. John's Hospital, Bruges: *2, 15*. Bridgeman Art Library, London (Christopher Wood Gallery, London *7*; National Museum of India, New Delhi *33*; Private Collection *35*; Historisches Museum Der Stadt, Vienna *60*; Prado, Madrid *101*; Gulbenkian Museum of Oriental Art, Durham *156*; Kunsthistorisches Museum, Vienna *191*). Bridgeman/Giraudon (Galerie Nationale, Palermo, Sicily *119*; Musee Des Beaux-Arts, Lille *127*). Yatri: *8, 46, 47, 49*. Comstock Photo Library, London: *9, 73, 75, 138, 172, 173, 195, 204, 211*. Bodleian Library, Oxford (Lincoln College, Oxford *10, 16, 17, 28, 41, 54, 63, 84, 86, 87, 93, 102, 110, 114, 124, 126, 129, 134* (top), *136, 143, 146, 159, 163, 165, 169, 170, 174, 176, 183, 200, 202, 203*); Bodleian Library, Oxford: *22, 23, 50, 58, 66, 70, 185*. Mary Evans Picture Library, London: *12*. Biblioteca Nacional, Madrid: *13, 30*. Impact Photos, London (Caroline Penn *14*; Robert Eames *26/7*; Ben Edwards *57*; John Cole *107*; David Reed *141*; Piers Cavendish *155*; Jeremy Nicholl *166*; Rupert Conant *180*; John Cole *181*). Irish National Library, Dublin: *18, 29*. Musee Conde, Paris: *20*. Beth Alpha Synagogue, Israel: *21*. Werner Forman Archive, London: *24, 25*. Ancient Art & Architecture, London: *34, 36, 89, 92, 103, 111, 184*. Viewfinder Colour Photo Library, Bristol: *38/9*, (Bob Whitfield *52*). Abbey of St. Hildegard, Germany: *40*. British Library, London: *43*. Turkish Embassy, London: *51, 53*. The Science Museum Picture Library, London: *55, 62, 67, 71, 81*. David Hoffman, London: *59*. The British Museum, London: *64, 88, 142*. Format Partners Photo Library, London: *65, 168*. Pat Hodgson Library, Surrey: *69*. Krishnamurti Foundation: *77, 167*. Osho Foundation International, India: *78, 120, 205*. Magnum Photos Ltd, London: *82, 91, 179*. Tate Gallery, London: *85, 131*. Imperial War Museum, London: *94, 98, 100*. Fitzwilliam Museum, Cambridge: *115*. Sygma Ltd, London: *117, 122/3, 135, 144, 149, 164*. Telegraph Colour Library, London: *125, 128, 133, 137, 148, 189*. National Gallery, London: *145*. Colorific Photo Library Ltd: *148*. Victoria & Albert Museum, London: *150* (top). National Portrait Gallery, London: *150* (bottom). Bibliotheque National, Paris: *151*. Labyrinth Collection: *152, 162*. Collections, London (Anthea Sieveking *153*,). Alinari, Italy: *157*. Rosenbach Foundation, Philadelphia: *158*. Images Colour Library Ltd, London: *161, 171, 177*. Image Bank, London (Don Landwehrle *175*). Topham Picture Source, Kent: *187, 190*. Robert McFarlane: *192*. National Trust Photo Library, London: *197*. Jean Williamson/Mick Sharp Photography, Wales: *198, 206/7*. Alexander Valentinovich, Moscow: *208*. St. Botolph's Vestry, London: *213*. Sir John Soane's Museum, London: *215*. St. Bavo's, Ghent: *216*